CONTENTS

CHAPTER 1

Introduction

Purpose of the practical guide

1.1 This consultation paper presents a draft Practical Guide to European Directive 2001/42/EC "on the assessment of the effects of certain plans and programmes on the environment", known as the Strategic Environmental Assessment or SEA Directive. The purpose of the Practical Guide is to provide key facts together with guidance on how to comply with the Directive in an environmental assessment of a plan or programme. The Guide is intended to apply to all plans and programmes in the UK which fall within the scope of the Directive. Specific guidance has however been developed for certain types of plans and programmes, particularly land use and spatial planning and transport planning (see paragraph 1.7 below). Readers should use the relevant specific guidance when preparing those types of plans and programmes.

1.2 The Office of the Deputy Prime Minister (ODPM) has overall responsibility for implementing the SEA Directive throughout the UK. However, responsibility for its application to plans and programmes in Scotland and Wales lies with the Devolved Administrations (the Scottish Executive and Welsh Assembly Government), and in Northern Ireland, with the Department of the Environment. The Practical Guide is being developed jointly by all four bodies.

1.3 The guidance in this publication on how to comply with the Directive is not intended as an interpretation of the law, but should be read in conjunction with the Directive and the Regulations which transpose it into UK law:

- *The Environmental Assessment of Plans and Programmes Regulations 2004,*

- *The Environmental Assessment of Plans and Programmes Regulations (Northern Ireland) 2004,*

- *The Environmental Assessment of Plans and Programmes (Scotland) Regulations 2004, and*

- *The Environmental Assessment of Plans and Programmes (Wales) Regulations 2004.*

The first of the above Regulations applies to any plan or programme which relates either solely to the whole or any part of England, or to England and any other part of the UK. Each of the regulations for Scotland, Wales and Northern Ireland applies to plans and programmes which relate solely to the whole or any part of Scotland, Wales or Northern Ireland.

1.4 This publication is intended to be used by those concerned with SEA in the UK where no specific guidance has been developed for their types of plans or programmes (para 1.7 below sets out the specific guidance that is available). Those concerned may include authorities which produce plans and programmes (termed "Responsible Authorities" in the Regulations); the authorities with environmental responsibilities which must be consulted under the Directive (the "Consultation Bodies", or in Scotland "Consultation Authorities"); other government bodies, including those with roles in oversight of plans or programmes; consultants and advisers involved in undertaking SEA; and all those who may be affected by or have an interest in plans or programmes, including members of the public, non-government organisations, businesses and developers.

1.5   The Guide includes sections on:

- Background and context of the Directive

- Consultation

- SEA and sustainable development

- The steps in the SEA process

The publication also includes answers to frequently asked questions, a glossary of SEA terms, a series of appendices on matters of detail, a Quality Assurance checklist, and the SEA Directive itself.

Other guidance on SEA

1.6   The European Commission has published guidance on the SEA Directive in *Implementation of Directive 2001/42 on the Assessment of the Effects of Certain Plans and Programmes on the Environment*. This provides useful advice on interpreting the terms used in the Directive, and is referred to below as "the European Commission guidance". It is available on the EU website: (http://europa.eu.int/comm/environment/eia/030923_sea_guidance.pdf)

1.7   UK guidance on the SEA Directive for specific types of plans and programmes includes:

- Land use and spatial plans in England (ODPM): The *SEA Directive: Guidance for Planning Authorities (www.odpm.gov.uk)* (also see para 1.8 below).

- Land use and spatial plans in Scotland (Scottish Executive): *Interim guidance on the Environmental Assessment of Development Plans (Scotland)* (www.scotland.gov.uk/library5/planning/eadp-00.asp)

- Transport plans in England (DfT): *Strategic Environmental Assessment – Core Guidance for Transport Plans [DfT] (www.dft.gov.uk)*

- Environment Agency Guidelines 2004: *SEA Good Practice Guidelines (Available during August at www.environment-agency.gov.uk/seaguidelines)*

1.8 New draft guidance on Sustainability Appraisal of Regional Spatial Strategies and Local Development Frameworks, incorporating the requirements of the SEA Directive, will be available for England in September.

1.9 The Welsh Assembly Government and the Department of Environment for Northern Ireland are developing SEA guidance for Welsh and Northern Irish planning authorities respectively.

Responding to this consultation document

1.10 Please note that responses to this consultation document should be received no later than 29th October 2004.

1.11 Responses, and any comments about this consultation, may either be sent to:

Sarah Sing, Office of the Deputy Prime Minister, PICA(E), 3/C1, Eland House, Bressenden Place, London SW1E 5DU (tel. 020 7944 5879; fax.no 020 7944 3899)

or

e-mailed to sarah.sing@odpm.gsi.gov.uk

Copies of the consultation document

1.12 Hard copies of this consultation document can be obtained from ODPM Free Literature, PO Box 236, Wetherby, West Yorkshire LS23 7NB (tel. 0870 1226 236; fax. 0870 1226 237; Textphone: 0870 120 7405; e-mail: odpm@twoten.press.net)

1.13 The consultation document is also available on the ODPM website: www.planning.odpm.gov.uk

1.14 A summary of responses to this consultation document will be published on the ODPM website no later than 21st January 2005. Hard copies of this summary may be obtained after that date from Sarah Sing at the address shown above. Unless you specifically state that your response, or any part of it, is confidential, we shall assume that you have no objection to its being made available to the public and identified on the ODPM website. Confidential responses will be included in any numerical summary or analysis of responses.

The consultation criteria

1.15 This consultation is being conducted in accordance with the Government's Code of Practice on Consultation. The criteria below apply to all UK national public consultations on the basis of a document in electronic or printed form. They will often be relevant to other sorts of consultation.

1.16 Though they have no legal force, and cannot prevail over statutory or other mandatory external requirements (e.g. under European Community Law), they should otherwise generally be regarded as binding on UK departments and their agencies, unless Ministers conclude that exceptional circumstances require a departure.

1. Consult widely throughout the process, allowing a minimum of 12 weeks for written consultation at least once during the development of the policy.

2. Be clear about what your proposals are, who may be affected, what questions are being asked and the timescale for responses.

3. Ensure that your consultation is clear, concise and widely accessible.

4. Give feedback regarding the responses received and how the consultation process influenced the policy.

5. Monitor your department's effectiveness at consultation, including through the use of a designated consultation co-ordinator.

6. Ensure your consultation follows better regulation best practice, including carrying out a Regulatory Impact Assessment if appropriate.

1.17   The full consultation code may be viewed at www.cabinet-office.gov.uk/regulation/Consultation/Introduction.htm

1.18   Are you satisfied that this consultation has followed these criteria? If not, or you have any other observations about ways of improving the consultation process please contact:

David Plant, ODPM Consultation Co-ordinator, Room 3.19, 26 Whitehall, London, SW1A 2WH; or by e-mail to: david.plant@odpm.gsi.gov.uk

Acknowledgements

1.19   This guidance draws extensively on the previous ODPM publication *The SEA Directive: Guidance for Planning Authorities*, prepared by Levett-Therivel Sustainability Consultants. It also draws on work for ODPM by Land Use Consultants and Collingwood Environmental Planning on aspects of sustainability appraisal in planning and on work by TRL on SEA of transport plans.

CHAPTER 2

Background and Context

Objectives and requirements

2.1   The objective of the Directive is "to provide for a high level of protection of the environment and to contribute to the integration of environmental considerations into the preparation and adoption of plans and programmes with a view to promoting sustainable development" (Article 1). These aims are consistent with a range of UK Government policies on the environment and sustainable development.

2.2   Though usually referred to as the SEA Directive, it does not use the term "strategic environmental assessment" or SEA; rather, it requires an "environmental assessment" of certain plans and programmes. For convenience however, **the term SEA is used in this guidance to mean an environmental assessment which complies with the Directive**.

2.3   The Directive defines "environmental assessment" as a procedure comprising:

-   preparing an Environmental Report on the likely significant effects of the draft plan or programme;

-   carrying out consultation on the draft plan or programme and the accompanying Environmental Report;

-   taking into account the Environmental Report and the results of consultation in decision making; and

-   providing information when the plan or programme is adopted and showing how the results of the environmental assessment have been taken into account.

2.4   The SEA must be carried out during the preparation of the plan or programme and before its adoption. Where a plan or programme is formally adopted by the passage of a law or regulations by legislative body such as Parliament, the SEA must be carried out before the proposal is submitted to the legislative procedure, but this is rare in the UK. Figure 1 sets out these requirements in detail, with references to the relevant provisions of the Directive.

The regulatory impact of the Directive

2.5   ODPM has provided information on the costs and benefits of implementing the SEA Directive in the UK. This information is available in the Regulatory Impact Assessment accompanying the *Environmental Assessment of Plans and Programmes Regulations 2004* on the ODPM website (www.odpm.gov.uk).

The Directive's field of application

2.6 Under Article 2(a), the plans and programmes subject to the Directive are those which are:

- subject to preparation and/or adoption by an authority at national, regional or local level, or are prepared by an authority for adoption through a legislative procedure by Parliament or Government, *and*

- required by legislative, regulatory or administrative provisions.

Typical characteristics of "administrative provisions" are that they are publicly available, prepared in a formal way, probably involving consultation with interested parties. The administrative provision must have sufficient formality such that it counts as a "provision" and it must also use language that plainly requires rather than just encourages a plan or programme to be prepared.

Figure 1 **The SEA Directive's requirements**	
Requirements	**Where covered in Guide (stage/ appendix)**
Preparation of an environmental report in which the likely significant effects on the environment of implementing the plan or programme, and reasonable alternatives taking into account the objectives and geographical scope of the plan or programme, are identified, described and evaluated. The information to be given is (Art. 5 and Annex I):	
a) An outline of the contents, main objectives of the plan or programme, and relationship with other relevant plans and programmes;	A
b) The relevant aspects of the current state of the environment and the likely evolution thereof without implementation of the plan or programme;	A
c) The environmental characteristics of areas likely to be significantly affected;	B and Appendices 4 and 5
d) Any existing environmental problems which are relevant to the plan or programme including, in particular, those relating to any areas of a particular environmental importance, such as areas designated pursuant to Directives 79/409/EEC and 92/43/EEC;	A
e) The environmental protection objectives, established at international, Community or national level, which are relevant to the plan or programme and the way those objectives and any environmental considerations have been taken into account during its preparation;	A
f) The likely significant effects on the environment, including on issues such as biodiversity, population, human health, fauna, flora, soil, water, air, climatic factors, material assets, cultural heritage including architectural and archaeological heritage, landscape and the interrelationship between the above factors. (Footnote: These effects should include secondary, cumulative, synergistic, short, medium and long-term permanent and temporary, positive and negative effects);	B, C
g) The measures envisaged to prevent, reduce and as fully as possible offset any significant adverse effects on the environment of implementing the plan or programme;	B, C
h) An outline of the reasons for selecting the alternatives dealt with, and a description of how the assessment was undertaken including any difficulties (such as technical deficiencies or lack of know-how) encountered in compiling the required information;	B, C
i) a description of measures envisaged concerning monitoring in accordance with Art. 10;	C, E
j) a non-technical summary of the information provided under the above headings	B, C

Requirements	Where covered in Guide (stage/ appendix)
The report must include the information that may reasonably be required taking into account current knowledge and methods of assessment, the contents and level of detail in the plan or programme, its stage in the decision-making process and the extent to which certain matters are more appropriately assessed at different levels in that process to avoid duplication of the assessment (Art. 5.2)	C
Consultation:	
• authorities with environmental responsibility, when deciding on the scope and level of detail of the information which must be included in the environmental report (Art. 5.4)	B and Section 3
• authorities with environmental responsibility and the public, shall be given an early and effective opportunity within appropriate time frames to express their opinion on the draft plan or programme and the accompanying environmental report before the adoption of the plan or programme (Art. 6.1, 6.2)	D and Section 3
• other EU Member States, where the implementation of the plan or programme is likely to have significant effects on the environment of that country (Art. 7).	D and Section 3
Taking the environmental report and the results of the consultations into account in decision-making (Art. 8)	D
Provision of information on the decision: When the plan or programme is adopted, the public and any countries consulted under Art.7 must be informed and the following made available to those so informed: • the plan or programme as adopted • a statement summarising how environmental considerations have been integrated into the plan or programme and how the environmental report of Article 5, the opinions expressed pursuant to Article 6 and the results of consultations entered into pursuant to Art. 7 have been taken into account in accordance with Art. 8, and the reasons for choosing the plan or programme as adopted, in the light of the other reasonable alternatives dealt with; and • the measures decided concerning monitoring (Art. 9)	D
Monitoring of the significant environmental effects of the plan's or programme's implementation (Art. 10)	E
Quality assurance: environmental reports should be of a sufficient standard to meet the requirements of the SEA Directive	QA checklist

2.7   Article 3(2) makes SEA mandatory for plans and programmes:

- which are prepared for agriculture, forestry, fisheries, energy, industry, transport, waste management, water management, telecommunications, tourism, town and country planning or land use and which set the framework for future development consent for projects listed in Annexes I and II to Directive 85/337/EEC (the Environmental Impact Assessment (EIA) Directive); or

- which, in view of the likely effect on sites, have been determined to require an assessment pursuant to Article 6 or 7 of Directive 92/43/EEC (the Habitats Directive)

2.8   Under Article 3(3) and (4), environmental assessment is only required for certain categories of plans and programmes where they are judged likely to have significant environmental effects. These are:

- Plans and programmes within the categories in Article 3(2a) which determine the use of small areas at local level, or are minor modifications to plans and programmes within this "core scope"

- Any plans and programmes outside this core scope which set the framework for future development consent of projects (not limited to projects listed in the Annexes to the EIA Directive)

2.9 Responsible Authorities should determine whether plans or programmes of the types covered by Article 3(3) and (4) are likely to have significant environmental effects, and hence whether SEA is required under the Directive. The Directive allows such screening by means of either case-by-case examination or by specifying types of plans and programmes, or by combining both approaches. Annex II of the Directive lists criteria for determining the likely significance of the environmental effects of plans or programmes, and these must be taken into account when screening. On determination of whether a plan or programme requires a SEA, the Responsible Authority must make information on the decision available to the public.

2.10 When forming a view on whether SEA is needed in these cases, Responsible Authorities must seek the views of specified authorities concerned with the environment (the Consultation Bodies). Section 4 gives more information on these bodies and their role.

2.11 The diagram at Appendix 1 of this guidance shows the Directive's criteria of application.

2.12 The SEA Directive applies to plans and programmes whose first formal preparatory act is after 21 July 2004, and also, with retroactive effect, to those which have not been either adopted or submitted to a legislative procedure leading to adoption by 21 July 2006.

Exemptions

2.13 Under Article 3(8), the Directive does not apply to:

- plans and programmes the sole purpose of which is to serve national defence or civil emergency

- financial or budget plans and programmes

- plans and programmes co-financed under the respective programming periods for Council Regulations EC 1260/1999 and EC 1257/1999 (on which programme spending continues until the end of 2008)

The Directive and SEA practice

2.14   Environmental assessment is already established practice for many types of plan and programme in the UK, but specific requirements and approaches vary. The Directive brings a new emphasis to the following areas in particular:

- Collecting and presenting baseline environmental information

- Predicting significant environmental effects of the plan or programme, including those of alternatives

- Addressing adverse environmental effects through mitigation measures

- Consulting the public and authorities with environmental responsibilities as part of the assessment process

- Monitoring the environmental effects of the plan or programme during its implementation

Who should do SEA?

2.15   The Directive does not prescribe who should carry out an SEA, but normally it is the responsibility of the authority which prepares the plan or programme.

2.16   Good practice in SEA emphasises that the assessment should be well integrated with the plan- or programme-making process. Many benefits of SEA may be lost if it is carried out as a completely separate work-stream or by a separate body. But it can be helpful to involve people, either within the Responsible Authority or outside, who are not directly concerned in producing the plan or programme and can contribute expertise or a detached and independent view.

CHAPTER 3

SEA and Consultation

Requirements for consultation

3.1 The Directive creates the following requirements on consultation:

- Authorities which, because of their environmental responsibilities, are likely to be concerned by the effects of implementing the plan or programme, must be consulted on the scope and level of detail of the information to be included in the Environmental Report. These authorities are designated in the Regulations as the Consultation Bodies (Consultation Authorities in Scotland).

- The public and the Consultation Bodies must be consulted on the draft plan or programme and the Environmental Report, and must be given an early and effective opportunity within appropriate time frames to express their opinions.

- Other EU Member States must be consulted if the plan or programme is likely to have significant effects on the environment in their territories.

- The Consultation Bodies must also be consulted on determinations on whether SEA is needed for plans or programmes under Article 3(5), i.e. those which may be excluded if they are not likely to have significant environmental effects.

3.2 The Directive requires responses to consultation to be taken into account during the preparation of the plan or programme and before its adoption or submission to a legislative procedure.

Figure 2: **Summary of consultation requirements under SEA Directive**		
Stage of SEA	Consultation requirements in Domestic situations	Additional requirements in Transboundary situations
Determination if a plan or programme or programme requires an SEA	Consult Consultation Bodies. Information made available to 'the public'.	
Decision on scope and level of detail of the assessment	Consult Consultation Bodies.	
Environmental report and draft plan or programme	Information made available to the public. Consult Consultation Bodies. Consult 'the public'.	Consultation of 'environmental authorities' in the Member State likely to be affected. Consultation of the public concerned in the Member State likely to be affected.
During preparation of plan or programme	Take account of Environmental Report and opinions expressed (and produce statement).	Take account of results of transboundary consultation.
Adopted plan or programme; statement and measures concerning monitoring	Information made available to Consultation Bodies. Information made available to 'the public'.	Information made available to the consulted Member State.

Adapted from EU (2003)

The Consultation Bodies

3.3   The designated Consultation Bodies in the UK are:

- England: Countryside Agency, English Heritage, English Nature, and the Environment Agency

- Northern Ireland: Department of the Environment

- Scotland: Historic Scotland, Scottish Natural Heritage, and the Scottish Environment Protection Agency

- Wales: Cadw (Welsh Historic Monuments), Countryside Council for Wales, and the Environment Agency Wales

3.4   The Consultation Bodies for England are developing a statement of the standards of service they will provide to Responsible Authorities (see box below).

SEA SERVICES FROM THE CONSULTATION BODIES FOR ENGLAND

The Government proposes to designate four consultation bodies for England – the Countryside Agency, English Heritage, English Nature and the Environment Agency as "authorities with environmental responsibility" in relation to the SEA Directive (also termed "consultation bodies" in the draft regulations), which must be consulted during the SEA assessment process.

The four Agencies are developing a common set of service standards which will set out the services and standards which plan-makers can expect when consulting them as part of a Strategic Environmental Assessment process (and in the case of Local Planning Authorities when conducting integrated SEA and Sustainability Appraisal).

The agencies are anticipating high volumes of SEA consultations, some of which will substitute for existing informal and formal consultation (e.g. as part of the Development Planning process), and some of which will be completely new. The service standards are intended as a guide to their own staff, to help with workload management, as well as to those bodies consulting them as part of SEA assessments. These standards are non-statutory and are provided only as a guide, although the intention is that agency staff will use their best endeavours to meet them.

The standards document is expected to describe:

- the general approach the agencies will take to deciding on their consultation response e.g. whether to provide a detailed reply or standing guidance, at which of the consultation stages they expect to focus their efforts.

- The particular interests, and expertise of each agency and the information they hold and therefore the different SEA topics on which they are likely to respond (the leaflet contains tables of agencies against SEA topics, and information held).

- Expected response times, and how each consultation type (screening, scoping, environmental report, decision to adopt) will be dealt with.

- A general summary of the type of advice which plan-makers may expect when consulting the agencies under each section of the Environmental Report (using the same headings as in the Draft SEA Regulations Schedule 2).

Consulting the public

3.5   The Directive defines "the public" as "one or more natural or legal persons and, in accordance with national legislation or practice, their associations, organisations or groups". It includes, but is not limited to, "the public affected or likely to be affected by, or having an interest in" a plan or programme, including relevant non-governmental organisations". It should also include appropriate government and stakeholder bodies such as local authorities and Regional Development Agencies.

3.6   It is for the Responsible Authority to identify the public to be consulted on a particular plan or programme and its Environmental Report. In addition to the Directive, the authority should naturally take account of any legal obligations or guidelines relevant to the plan or programme for which it is responsible.

3.7   When carrying out consultation, Responsible Authorities should have regard to:

- The agreement between Government and the voluntary sector, the *Compact Code of Good Practice on Community Groups*, which sets out agreed ways of working with community groups and voluntary organisations including black and ethnic minority groups and organisations (see http://www.thecompact.org.uk.)

- The *Race Relations (Amendment) Act 2000* to promote race equality and the *Disability Act 1995* to ensure that disabled people are not discriminated against.

- The Cabinet Office *Code of Practice on Consultation* which sets out criteria for conducting effective consultation. UK non-departmental public bodies and local authorities are encouraged to follow this code.

3.8   The Audit Commission has issued briefing on effective community consultation (*Listen Up!*) which sets out a comprehensive range of consultation techniques with advice on how they can be used, their advantages, disadvantages, and resource implications – see References for details.

Practical aspects of consultation

3.9   Timing of consultation should be built into the preparations for the plan or programme and the Environmental Report from the start, to maximise the prospect of improving the proposals concerned, and so that sufficient time is left for it at each stage

3.10   It may be helpful to produce an outline of how consultation is to be conducted, making clear how the Directive's requirements will be met (normally as part of the wider consultation strategy for the plan or programme). The strategy should indicate the objectives of the consultation process, what consultation activities will be conducted, what information and documents will be made available, how they can be obtained, how consultation responses will be considered, and how the Responsible Authority will provide feedback to consultees. It may be beneficial to involve a selection of consultees in the development of this outline.

3.11   To be effective, consultation needs to be undertaken by people with the right skills, knowledge and experience. While consultation can be managed with the assistance of experts, Responsible Authorities are encouraged to build the capacity of their SEA teams to conduct consultation.

3.12   The form of consultation and the participation of individuals and organisations will vary depending on the nature and scale of the plan or programme. It is for example often difficult for local representative groups to take a regional perspective, when their work and interests are focused on a particular locality. Similarly, bodies represented at the regional level may not always be familiar with local issues. It is important to ensure that participants are involved at appropriate levels. This can also help to reduce the amount of involvement that different interests are invited to participate in and to avoid the problems of "consultation fatigue".

3.13 Some consultees may not want to become active participants. They may only wish to be kept informed, or to be involved in a broader sense through participatory events or written consultation. Others will want to take a more active role. Much depends on the measures used to encourage their interest and involvement. It is important to be aware that stakeholders are not a homogenous group and to allow them to indicate how they wish to be involved. Lists of stakeholders will typically expand and change as the SEA process progresses and new issues emerge or issues cease to be relevant.

3.14 A plan or programme prepared wholly within one part of the UK (e.g. England) may nonetheless have significant effects in another part (e.g. Scotland or Wales). In such cases the Responsible Authority should make arrangements to consult the Consultation Bodies and the public in the areas affected.

Transboundary consultation with EU Member States

3.15 Where a plan or programme is likely to have significant effects on the environment in another Member State of the European Union, the Directive makes provision for transboundary consultation. This will normally be co-ordinated centrally, and separate guidance will be issued on the practical arrangements. Where a Responsible Authority expects a plan or programme to need transboundary consultation, it should bear in mind the time needed for contact to be established between the government bodies concerned, the identification of and consultation with the public and environmental authorities in the affected Member State, and consideration of the resulting comments.

CHAPTER 4

SEA and Sustainable Development

4.1 The objectives of the SEA Directive include the promotion of sustainable development. This section outlines what this means in the UK context.

4.2 The UK Government published a Sustainable Development Strategy in 1999 which defines the aim of sustainable development as "ensuring a better quality of life for everyone, now and for generations to come". Achieving this means meeting the following four objectives *at the same time*, in the UK and the world as a whole.

- social progress which recognises the needs of everyone;

- effective protection of the environment;

- prudent use of natural resources; and

- maintenance of high and stable levels of economic growth and employment.

No one of these objectives is more important than another. Although there can be tensions between them, in the long term success in one is dependent on the others.

4.3 The Northern Ireland Executive and National Assembly for Wales have both endorsed this approach, and the National Assembly has also described sustainable development more simply, saying that we should treat the Earth as though we intend to stay.

4.4 The Scottish Executive describes the basic aim of sustainable development as securing the future, acknowledging that achieving economic growth has to be done in such a way that it does not harm the environment or squander the natural resources we depend on, and having to distribute the wealth it creates to improve quality of life and to eradicate poverty.

4.5 By 2005 the Government aims to have in place a new strategy that will provide a strong basis for renewed action to deliver sustainable development. A strategic framework for sustainable development to 2020 will be agreed by the UK Government and the administrations in Scotland, Wales and Northern Ireland, to provide a consistent approach and focus across the UK. There will also be separate strategies by each administration, building on existing work and also translating the framework into action, based on their different responsibilities, needs and views.

4.6 Responsible Authorities are free to broaden the scope of the assessment to include social and economic effects of their plans and programmes in addition to environmental effects. When seeking to integrate SEA with appraisal of other types of effect, it may be helpful to seek:

- Opportunities to optimise information collection processes so that information collected can be used to satisfy all appraisal requirements

- Consistency amongst objectives used

- Compatibility of information generated through forecasting and prediction techniques to generate comparable results between social, economic and environmental information

- Integrating staging of assessment to create a single process wherever possible, taking advantage of synergies

- Facilitating transparency in decision making through analysis techniques that generate comparable findings

- Implementing a consistent level of rigour throughout assessment and appraisal

CHAPTER 5

Stages of SEA

Introduction

5.1   This section gives stage-by-stage advice on the Directive's requirements, the decisions to be taken and the documentation to be provided. More detailed information on specific aspects of SEA is given in the Appendices.

5.2   These stages are intended to be valid for all plans and programmes to which the Directive applies, whatever their sector or geographical scope. However, where specific guidance is available for certain types of plans and programmes, readers should use the stages set out in that guidance (see para 1.7 above). In practice SEA should always be adapted to the scale and nature of the plan or programme in question, its place in any hierarchy or sequence of plans or programmes, and the stage reached in the decision-making process.

5.3   The SEA process, including preparation of the Environmental Report, should start as early as possible, and ideally at the same time as the preparation of the plan or programme. SEA will often involve an iterative process of collecting information, defining alternatives, identifying environmental effects, developing mitigation measures and revising proposals in the light of predicted environmental effects. Figure 3 summarises the main stages in the SEA process and the purpose of each stage. Stages B and C are particularly likely to be iterative. It will be important to identify an end-point where further iterations are unlikely to bring further significant improvements in the environmental effects of the plan or programme.

Figure 3. **Stages in the SEA Process**	
SEA stages and tasks	**Purpose**
Stage A: Setting the context and establishing the baseline	
Identifying other relevant plans, programmes and environmental protection objectives	To document how the plan/programme is affected by outside factors and suggest ideas for how any constraints can be addressed. Help to identify SEA objectives.
Collecting baseline information	To provide an evidence base for environmental problems, effects prediction and monitoring. Also help in the development of SEA objectives
Identifying environmental problems	To help focus the SEA and streamline the subsequent stages including baseline information analysis, setting of the SEA objectives, prediction of effects and monitoring
Developing SEA objectives	To provide a means by which the environmental performance of the plan or programme can be assessed
Stage B: Deciding the scope of SEA and developing strategic alternatives	
Testing the plan or programme objectives against the SEA objectives	To ensure that the overall objectives of the plan or programme are in accordance with the SEA objectives and provide a suitable framework for developing options
Appraising strategic alternatives	To assist in the development and refinement of the strategic alternative by identifying potential environmental impacts of alternatives for achieving the plan or programme objectives
Consulting on the scope of SEA	To ensure the SEA covers the key environmental issues
Stage C: Assessing the effects of the plan or programme.	
Predicting the effects of the plan or programme, including alternatives	To predict the significant environmental effects of the plan or programme and its alternatives
Evaluating the effects of the plan or programme, including alternatives	To evaluate the predicted effects of the plan or programme and its alternatives and assist in the refinement of the plan or programme
Mitigating adverse effects	To ensure all potential mitigation measures are considered and as a result residual effects are identified
Proposing measures to monitor the environmental effects of plan or programme implementation	To detail the means by which the environmental performance of the plan or programme can be assessed
Preparing the Environmental Report	To provide a detailed account of the SEA process, including the findings of the environmental assessment and how it influenced the development of the draft plan or programme, in a format suitable for public consultation and decision-makers

Figure 3. **Stages in the SEA Process**

SEA stages and tasks	Purpose
Stage D: Consulting and decision-making	
Consulting on the draft plan or programme and the Environmental Report	To provide the public and Consultation Bodies with an opportunity to express their opinions on the findings of the Environmental Report and to use it as a reference point in commenting on the strategy or plan or programme. To gather more information on the baselines and environmental problems through the opinions and concerns of the public and identify preferred alternatives.
Assessment of significant changes	To ensure that any significant changes to the draft plan or programme are assessed for their environmental implications and influence the revision of the draft plan or programme.
Decision making and provision of information	To provide information on how the Environment Report and consultees opinions were taken into account in preparing the plan or programme
Stage E: Monitoring implementation of the plan or programme	
Developing aims and methods for monitoring	To measure the environmental performance of the plan or programme in order to determine whether its effects are as anticipated, and thereby inform future revisions
Responding to adverse effects	Ensure that adverse effects can be identified and appropriate responses developed

Stage A: Setting the context and establishing the baseline

WHAT THE DIRECTIVE SAYS:

The Environmental Report should provide information on:

- "the relationship [of the plan or programme] with other relevant plans and programmes" (Annex I(a))

- "the environmental protection objectives, established at international, [European] Community or national level, which are relevant to the plan or programme ... and the way those objectives and any environmental considerations have been taken into account during its preparation" (Annex I (a), (e))

- "relevant aspects of the current state of the environment and the likely evolution thereof without implementation of the plan or programme" and "the environmental characteristics of the areas likely to be significantly affected" (Annex I (b), (c))

- "any existing environmental problems which are relevant to the plan or programme including, in particular, those relating to any areas of a particular environmental importance, such as areas designated pursuant to Directives 79/409/EEC and 92/43/EEC" (Annex I (c))

5.A.1   At this stage the Responsible Authority compiles the background information needed for an SEA. To get the full benefit of integrating SEA into the plan or programme preparation process, this material is needed at the outset, when issues are being identified and alternative options are being developed.

5.A.2   Responsible Authorities should consider what information they already have and what more they will need. They may already hold useful information, for example from environmental assessments of previous plans or programmes. It may be useful to consult other bodies and the public at this stage to seek information and initial opinions.

Much baseline information will be generic to an area or sector, rather than specific to the particular plan or programme on which SEA is being carried out. It could therefore be used to support assessments of a range of plans or programmes prepared by one or more authorities. These potential uses and opportunities for information sharing and collaboration should be kept in mind when information is collected. To get the best value from the information, it should be kept up to date. It should not be merely a snapshot of the situation at a particular time.

IDENTIFYING OTHER RELEVANT PLANS, PROGRAMMES AND ENVIRONMENTAL PROTECTION OBJECTIVES

5.A.3   A plan or programme may be influenced in various ways by other plans or programmes, or by external environmental protection objectives such as those laid down in policies or legislation. Environmental assessments conducted in the preparation of other relevant plans and programmes are also likely to be useful sources of information. These relationships should be identified to enable the Responsible Authority to take advantage of potential synergies and to deal with any inconsistencies and constraints.

5.A.4   Some issues may already have been dealt with in other plans and programmes, and need not be addressed further in the plan or programme which is being developed. Where significant tensions or inconsistencies arise, however, it may be helpful to consider principles of precedence between levels or types of plan or programme; the relative timing of the plans or programmes concerned; the degree to which the plans, programmes and objectives accord with current policy or legal requirements; and the extent of any environmental assessments which have already been conducted.

> **Appendix 2** gives an indicative list of plans, programmes and environmental protection objectives which may be relevant.

5.A.5   The results of this exercise can be documented as a table such as Figure 4 which shows the requirements of the other plans, programmes or objectives concerned, the constraints or challenges they pose, and how the plan or programme might take account of them.

Figure 4. **Possible approach to documenting links with other relevant plans and programmes or environmental protection objectives**		
Other plan/programme	Objectives or requirements of the other plan or programme	How objectives and requirements might be taken on board

COLLECTING BASELINE INFORMATION

5.A.6   Baseline information provides the basis for predicting and monitoring environmental effects and helps to identify environmental problems and alternative ways of dealing with them. Sufficient information about the current and likely future state of the environment should be collected to allow the plan's or programme's effects to be adequately predicted.

5.A.7   For each indicator selected, enough information should be collected to answer the following questions:

- How good or bad is the current situation? Do trends show that it is getting better or worse?

- How far is the current situation from any established thresholds or targets?

- Are particularly sensitive or important elements of the receiving environment affected, e.g. people, resources, species, habitats?

- Are the problems reversible or irreversible, permanent or temporary?

- How difficult would it be to offset or remedy any damage?

- Have there been significant cumulative or synergistic effects over time? Are there expected to be such effects in the future?

> **Appendix 4** lists some key sources for baseline information.
> **Appendix 5** suggests how baseline information can be presented.

> In theory, collection of baseline information could go on indefinitely. A practical approach is essential. Set a time limit for information collection. Do not expect to be able to obtain all relevant information in the first SEA of a plan or programme, but make arrangements to fill any major gaps for future replacements or reviews of plans or programmes.

5.A.8   Where baseline information is unavailable or unsatisfactory, Responsible Authorities should consider how they could improve it for use in assessments of future plans or programmes. Monitoring information collated during the implementation of various plans and programmes has the potential to be a valuable source of baseline information. The need for better information will be an important consideration when deciding how to monitor the implementation of the plan or programme – see Stages C, D and E below.

IDENTIFYING ENVIRONMENTAL PROBLEMS

5.A.9   Responsible Authorities will be aware of many environmental problems which they currently face. It may however be useful to look for potential problems, e.g. where there are tensions between current or future baseline conditions and existing objectives, targets or obligations. Identifying environmental problems is an opportunity to define key plan or programme issues and improve plan or programme objectives and alternatives.

DEVELOPING SEA OBJECTIVES

5.A.10   While not specifically required by the Directive, SEA objectives are a recognised way of considering the environmental effects of a plan or programme and comparing the effects of alternatives. They are distinct from the objectives of the plan or programme, though they may in some cases overlap with them. For example, a Responsible Authority may wish to avoid particular adverse environmental effects or enhance beneficial ones in the course of achieving the objectives of the plan or programme. SEA objectives can include both externally imposed environmental protection objectives laid down by law or policy and others devised specifically in relation to the context of the plan or programme.

5.A.11   Objectives can be expressed in the form of targets, the achievement of which is measurable using indicators. Appendix 3 gives information on devising SEA objectives, and targets and indicators based on them.

5.A.12   They can be revised as baseline information is collected and environmental problems identified, and can be used in monitoring the implementation of the plan or programme. However, state of the environment indicators are not always applicable. Instead the indicators should help the decision-making process and may not necessarily be the same during the assessment as in monitoring.

> SEA objectives and indicators should be developed in consultation with the Consultation Bodies and relevant stakeholders, and revisited in the light of the baseline information and any problems identified.

Stage B: Deciding the scope of SEA and developing alternatives

> **WHAT THE DIRECTIVE SAYS:**
>
> The Environmental Report should consider "reasonable alternatives taking into account the objectives and the geographical scope of the plan or programme" and give "an outline of the reasons for selecting the alternatives dealt with" (Article 5.1 and Annex I (h))
>
> "Authorities which, by reason of their specific environmental responsibilities, are likely to be concerned by the environmental effects of implementing plans and programmes ... shall be consulted when deciding on the scope and level of detail of the information which must be included in the environmental report" (Article 5.4).

5.B.1   At this stage, the Responsible Authority decides the scope of the Environmental Report, what alternatives and types of effect to assess, and what level of detail to present. The advice of the Consultation Bodies will be sought on the scope of the Environmental Report. Elements of Stage B may need to be carried out more than once in the course of a plan's or programme's development.

> While the activities at Stage A can be carried out before work begins on the plan or programme, those at Stage B are integral to the plan or programme preparation process and cannot be done effectively in isolation from it.

TESTING THE PLAN OR PROGRAMME OBJECTIVES AGAINST THE SEA OBJECTIVES

5.B.2   The objectives of the plan or programme may be tested against the SEA objectives to identify both potential synergies and inconsistencies. This information can help in developing alternatives during the development of the plan or programme, and may in some cases help to refine the objectives of the plan or programme itself. Where a plan or programme has several objectives it may also be helpful to test them against each other, as consistencies may give rise to adverse environmental effects.

5.B.3   The compatibility of the plan or programme objectives with each other and with SEA objectives can be tested using a framework such as that shown in Figure 9.

APPRAISING STRATEGIC ALTERNATIVES

5.B.4   The Directive does not create a specific requirement to put forward alternatives, but it is normal practice when developing a plan or programme to propose different ways of fulfilling its objectives. In the UK the term "options" is often used. Each alternative can be tested against the SEA objectives. Positive as well as negative effects should be considered, and uncertainties about the nature and significance of effects should be noted. This will often be an iterative process, with the alternatives being revised to enhance positive effects and reduce negative ones.

Appendix 7 gives more detail on identifying and comparing alternatives.

5.B.5   At this stage it may be possible to drop some alternatives from further consideration. Reasons for eliminating alternatives should be documented. Where necessary, Responsible Authorities should also document why they have not considered alternatives which might appear attractive or practicable. Justifications for these choices should be robust, as they can affect decisions on major developments.

5.B.6   It is not the purpose of the SEA to decide which alternative should be chosen for the plan or programme. This is the role of the decision-makers who have to make choices on the plan or programme to be adopted. The SEA simply provides information on the relative environmental performance of alternatives.

5.B.7   Throughout this part of the assessment, it may be necessary to revisit earlier tasks such as the collection of baseline information, as new information and issues emerge.

CONSULTING ON THE SCOPE OF SEA

5.B.8   Responsible Authorities must seek the views of the Consultation Bodies on the scope and level of detail of the Environmental Report. Consultation at this stage helps to ensure that the Report will be robust enough to support the plan or programme during the later stages of full public consultation. Responsible Authorities may also find it useful to consult with other organisations and individuals concerned at this stage to obtain information and opinions.

5.B.9   The Consultation Bodies are developing principles and procedures for handling scoping inquiries. It is for Responsible Authorities to establish how best to approach the Consultation Bodies in any particular case, but if possible it is recommended that they should aim to produce a draft or outline of the Environmental Report. (See Figure 6 on the content of Environmental Reports.)

5.B.10   The Directive does not require full consultation with the public until the Environmental Report on the draft plan or programme is finalised (see Stage D). But, depending on the nature and stage of development of the plan or programme, Responsible Authorities may find it useful to undertake wider consultation and/or make environmental information available during Stage B. This can help to inform discussion at this stage, and feedback from organisations or the public may also provide more information or highlight new issues for the Environmental Report.

Stage C. Assessing the effects of the plan or programme

WHAT THE DIRECTIVE SAYS:

In the Environmental Report, "the likely significant effects on the environment of implementing the plan or programme ... and reasonable alternatives ... are [to be] identified, described and evaluated" (Article 5.1). The Environmental Report should include information that may "reasonably be required taking into account current knowledge and methods of assessment, the contents and level of detail in the plan or programme [and] its stage in the decision-making process" (Article 5.2).

Information to be provided in the Environmental Report includes:

- "the likely significant effects on the environment, including on issues such as biodiversity, population, human health, fauna, flora, soil, water, air, climatic factors, material assets, cultural heritage, including architectural and archaeological heritage, landscape and the interrelationship between the above factors. These effects should include secondary, cumulative, synergistic, short, medium and long-term, permanent and temporary, positive and negative effects" (Annex I (f) and footnote)

- "an outline of the reasons for selecting the alternatives dealt with" (Annex I (h))

- "the measures envisaged to prevent, reduce and as fully as possible offset any significant adverse effects on the environment of implementing the plan or programme..." (Annex I (g))

5.C.1   Responsible Authorities should seek to predict and evaluate the effects of elements of the evolving plan or programme, including alternatives, while they are working on them. Where adverse effects are seen to be likely, possibilities for mitigation should be considered. Aspects of Stage C may need to be carried out more than once in the course of a plan's or programme's development.

PREDICTING THE EFFECTS OF THE PLAN OR PROGRAMME, INCLUDING ALTERNATIVES

5.C.2   Prediction of effects involves:

- Identifying the changes to the environmental baseline which are predicted to arise from the plan or programme, including alternatives. These can be compared with each other, with the "no plan or programme" or "business as usual" scenarios, and against the SEA objectives. Note that "no plan or programme" and "business as usual" scenarios can still involve changes to the baseline.

- Describing these changes in terms of their magnitude, their geographical scale, the time period over which they will occur, whether they are permanent or temporary, positive or negative, probable or improbable, frequent or rare, and whether or not there are secondary, cumulative and/or synergistic effects.

5.C.3   Predictions do not have to be expressed in quantitative terms. Hard data may enable Responsible Authorities or expert advisers to make detailed quantitative predictions, and this can be particularly useful where a plan's or programme's effects are uncertain, close to a threshold, or cumulative. But quantification is not always practicable, and broad-based and qualitative predictions can be equally valid and appropriate. As in current practice, these may be expressed in easily understood terms such as "getting better or worse" or a scale from ++ (very positive) to – – (very negative). It can be useful to link predictions to specific objectives, e.g. "will the plan or programme promote change in a desired direction?".

5.C.4   However, qualitative should not mean "guessed". Predictions should be supported by evidence, such as references to any research, discussions or consultation which helped those carrying out the SEA to reach their conclusions. The Environmental Report should document any uncertainties or limitations in the information underlying both qualitative and quantitative predictions. Assumptions, for instance about underlying trends or details of projects to be developed under the plan or programme, should be clearly stated.

5.C.5   Where a plan or programme includes proposals for individual projects, these should be assessed in sufficient level to enable significant environmental effects to be broadly predicted. Where Environmental Impact Assessment is needed later for the project, it is likely to be informed by the findings of the SEA, but it will not usually be appropriate or even possible to provide the level of detail needed for EIA in the context of the plan or programme.

> **Appendix 6** discusses how secondary, cumulative and synergistic effects can be addressed.

EVALUATING THE EFFECTS OF THE PLAN OR PROGRAMME, INCLUDING ALTERNATIVES

5.C.6   Evaluation involves forming a judgement on whether or not a predicted effect will be environmentally significant. The criteria of significance in Annex II of the Directive are relevant when considering a specific effect, e.g. its scale and permanence and the nature and sensitivity of the receiving environment. It may also be helpful to refer to the baseline information and indicators defined at Stage A.

5.C.7   Figure 5 suggests a format for integrating the prediction and evaluation of effects and summarising the findings of this stage. This is derived from established practice, but puts more emphasis on mitigation and enhancement measures. Appendix 9 explains how to fill out this table.

5.C.8   When filling in Figure 5, the SEA team should consider, for each alternative presented:

- Is it clear exactly what is proposed, and how the alternatives differ from each other or relate to the plan or programme as a whole?

- Is each alternative likely to have a significant adverse effect in relation to each of the environmental objectives or targets from Stage A?

- If so, can the effect be avoided or its severity reduced?

- If the effect cannot be avoided, e.g. by conditions or changes to the way it is implemented, can the alternative be changed or eliminated?

- If its effect is uncertain, or depends on how the plan or programme is implemented, how can this uncertainty be reduced?

The point of the assessment is not to fill in the table, but to ensure that the option, policy or proposal is as environmentally beneficial or sustainable as possible. The table is only a tool for doing this.

Figure 5. Illustration of documentation of effects.

SEA objectives	Targets (where available)	Can the effect be quantified? (if yes, insert data)	Effects over time 0= Neutral effect += positive effect - = negative effect			Comments/ explanation (e.g. significance, reversibility etc.)
			short term	medium term	long term	
Protect biodiversity at ecosystem, species and genetic levels	10% increase per 10 year period in sites with land managed to wildlife		0	+	++	
Promote positive health related behaviour	10% increase in children walking or cycling to school by 2007		0	+	+	
Increase levels of public transport accessibility	all homes to be within 400m of a bus stop by 2007	Yes, surveys of 'pedsheds'	-	0	++	
Additional information on changes to the option, proposals for mitigation, etc:						

Appendix 8 gives further guidance on prediction and evaluation of effects

---

5.C.9 The Directive also requires the analysis of effects to include "short, medium and long-term, permanent and temporary ... effects" (Annex I(f)). Effects may vary over different timescales; for example, public transport infrastructure may have serious adverse effects in the short term but positive ones in the long term. The timescales themselves will also vary depending on the type of plan or programme and the alternatives being considered. For air pollution, for instance, the short, medium and long terms could be 3, 10 and 25 years, while for climate change they could be 5, 20 and 100 years. Figure 5 allows short, medium and long timescales to be differentiated and specified as appropriate for particular types of effect.

MITIGATING ADVERSE EFFECTS

5.C.10 Annex I of the Directive requires the Environmental Report to include measures to prevent, reduce or offset any significant adverse effects that implementing the plan or programme is expected to have on the environment. For convenience, these measures are referred to in this guidance as "mitigation measures", but this should be understood to include proactive avoidance of adverse effects as well as actions taken after effects are noticed. Proactive avoidance of adverse effects and enhanced or beneficial effects should be considered in preparation of plans and programmes. Mitigation is one of the key outputs of the SEA. Proposals for mitigation measures should be documented in the Environment Report with their potential significant environmental effects (see C1 and C2).

5.C.11 Mitigation can take a wide range of forms, including:

- Changes to the alternative concerned, or to the plan or programme as a whole

- Technical measures to be applied during the implementation stage, e.g. buffer zones, application of design principles

- Identifying issues to be addressed in project environmental impact assessments for certain projects or classes of projects

- Proposals for changing other plans and programmes

PROPOSING MEASURES TO MONITOR THE ENVIRONMENTAL EFFECTS OF PLAN OR PROGRAMME IMPLEMENTATION

5.C.12 The significant environmental effects of the implementation of plans and programmes must be monitored to identify any unforeseen adverse effects and to enable appropriate remedial action to be taken (though the Directive does not create any obligations concerning remediation). Decisions on what to monitor and how to do it should be considered early in the SEA process and throughout the course of preparing the plan or programme. Stage E includes further guidance on developing aims and methods for monitoring.

PREPARING THE ENVIRONMENTAL REPORT

5.C.13 The Environmental Report is a key output of SEA. It should reflect and support the "draft plan or programme", the Directive's term for the plan or programme on which formal public consultation is carried out. Annex I of the Directive lists the information to be provided in the Environmental Report. Figure 6 proposes a structure for the Environmental Report.

5.C.14 While the Environment Report does not need to be issued as a separate document from the draft plan or programme, it must be clearly distinguishable from it. An Environmental Report may be included within a document covering effects other than those on the environment, for example as part of a Sustainability Appraisal. Where this is done, the document should clearly show that the Directive's requirements in relation to the Environmental Report have been met. This could be achieved through signposting the place or places in the document where the information required by the Directive is provided.

5.C.15   In deciding the length and the level of detail to be provided in an Environmental Report, the Responsible Authority should bear in mind its purpose as a public consultation document. It is likely to be of interest to a wide variety of readers, including decision-makers, other plan/programme-making practitioners, statutory consultees, NGOs, and members of the public. It should be written and prepared with this range of users in mind, and should include a non-technical summary. A Quality Assurance checklist is provided in this guidance to help Responsible Authorities ensure that the quality of the Report is sufficient to meet the requirements of the Directive

Figure 6. **Possible structure and contents of the Environmental Report**	
Structure of report	**Information to include**
Summary	• Non-technical summary • Statement on the difference the process has made • How to comment on the report
Methodology used	• Approach adopted in the SEA • Who was consulted, and when
Background	• Purpose of the SEA • Plan or programme objectives
SEA objectives and baseline and context	• Links to other international, national, regional and local plans and programmes, and relevant environmental objectives including how these have been taken into account • Description of baseline characteristics and predicted future baseline • Environmental issues and problems • Difficulties in collecting information, limitations of the data, assumptions made etc. • SEA objectives, targets and indicators
Plan/Programme issues and alternatives	• Main strategic alternatives considered and how they were identified • Comparison of the significant environmental effects of the alternatives • How environmental issues were considered in choosing the preferred strategic alternatives • Other alternatives considered and why they were rejected • Any proposed mitigation measures
Plan or programme policies	• Significant environmental effects of the policies and proposals • How environmental problems were considered in developing the policies and proposals • Proposed mitigation measures • Uncertainties and risks
Implementation	• Links to other tiers of plans and programmes and the project level (environmental impact assessment, design guidance etc.) • Proposals for monitoring

Stage D: Consulting and decision-making

> **WHAT THE DIRECTIVE SAYS:**
>
> "The authorities [with relevant environmental responsibilities] and the public...
> shall be given an early and effective opportunity within appropriate time frames
> to express their opinion on the draft plan or programme... and the
> accompanying Environmental Report before the adoption of the plan or
> programme" (Article 6(2)).
>
> "The environmental report, ... the opinions expressed [by consultees] and the
> results of any transboundary consultations ... shall be taken into account during
> the preparation of the plan or programme... and before its adoption..." (Article 8).
>
> "When a plan or programme ... is adopted, the [environmental] authorities [and]
> the public ... are informed and the following items [shall be] made available to
> those so informed: (a) the plan or programme ... as adopted, (b) a statement
> summarising how environmental considerations have been integrated into the
> plan or programme....including the reasons for choosing the plan or programme
> or programme as adopted, in light of other reasonable alternatives dealt with ...
> and (c) the measures decided concerning monitoring" (Article 9(1)).

CONSULTING ON THE DRAFT PLAN OR PROGRAMME AND ENVIRONMENTAL REPORT

5.D.1   The Environmental Report should be made available at the same time as the draft
plan or programme, as an integral part of the consultation process, and the
relationship between the two documents should be clearly indicated.

5.D.2   Publication of proposals and consultation on them are already established practice
for many plans and programmes, and are in many cases legal requirements. The
timing of consultation is however also important. Responsible Authorities must
ensure that the public and the Consultation Bodies are given "an early and effective
opportunity within appropriate time frames to express their opinion".

> **Section 3** above provides more detailed guidance on consulting the
> Consultation Bodies and the public as part of SEA.

ASSESSMENT OF SIGNIFICANT CHANGES

5.D.3   Where plans or programmes go thorough several successive consultation exercises,
the implications for the Environmental Report must be kept under review to ensure
that it remains consistent with the plan or programme on which opinions are being
sought. If significant changes are made from the original proposals, the Responsible
Authority should consider whether a revised Report is needed.

DECISION MAKING AND PROVISION OF INFORMATION

5.D.4   The Directive requires the information in the Environmental Report and the responses to consultation to be taken into account during the preparation of the plan or programme and before the final decision is taken to adopt it. Responsible Authorities should produce a summary of how they have taken these findings into account, and how environmental considerations more generally have been integrated into the plan or programme. This summary should provide enough information to make clear how the plan or programme was changed as a result of information in the Environmental Report or responses to consultation, or why no changes were made. It should also show why alternatives were rejected.

5.D.5   Information must also be made available on how monitoring will be carried out during implementation. This could conveniently be included in the summary of how the SEA was taken into account. The Environmental Report will already have documented proposed monitoring measures, and they can now be confirmed or modified in the light of consultation responses.

5.D.6   The Directive requires the plan or programme itself, when adopted, to be made available to the public, the Consultation Bodies, and EU Member States where these have been consulted. This guidance assumes that all plans and programmes in the UK which are subject to the Directive are freely available under existing legal provisions or policy. Responsible Authorities should however ensure that arrangements are in place to inform the public and other consultees that the plan or programme has been adopted, and to give them access to it if they are not provided with copies.

Stage E. Monitoring implementation of the plan or programme

WHAT THE DIRECTIVE SAYS:

"Member States shall monitor the significant environmental effects of the implementation of plans and programmes... in order, inter alia, to identify at an early stage unforeseen adverse effects, and to be able to undertake appropriate remedial action" (Article 10.1).

The Environmental Report should provide information on "a description of the measures envisaged concerning monitoring" (Annex I (i)).

5.E.1   Monitoring allows the actual significant environmental effects of implementing the plan or programme to be tested against those predicted. It thus helps to ensure that any problems which arise during implementation, whether or not they were foreseen, can be identified and future predictions made more accurately. It can also be used to compile baseline information for future plans and programmes, and to prepare information which will be needed for Environmental Impact Assessments of projects.

Appendix 9 gives more information on monitoring.

DEVELOPING AIMS AND METHODS FOR MONITORING

5.E.2   The Directive's provisions on monitoring apply when the plan or programme is being put into effect, rather than during its preparation and adoption. But preparations for monitoring should not be treated as a separate exercise from the rest of the SEA. Decisions on what to monitor and how to do it should always be considered in the course of preparing the plan or programme. Appendix 9 describes how Responsible Authorities may go about designing an SEA monitoring system.

5.E.3   In many cases, information used in monitoring will be provided by outside bodies, including those which provide baseline information (see Appendix 4). Responsible Authorities should take care to ensure that monitoring information is appropriate to their needs and is up to date and reliable. Proposals for and reports or other outputs from monitoring should state the sources of the information.

5.E.4   Monitoring in accordance with the Directive can be incorporated into existing monitoring arrangements. However, if monitoring is not already established under arrangements for implementing a plan or programme, a new procedural step for carrying it out will be required.

RESPONDING TO ADVERSE EFFECTS

5.E.5   Responsible Authorities should consider how they could react if monitoring reveals adverse effects. While the Directive itself does not create new obligations on environmental protection, other legislation or policies may require action on the part of either the Responsible Authority or another body. Details of any contingency arrangements could be included in the mitigation measures set out in the Environmental Report.

5.E.6   Figure 7 shows a possible format for documenting a proposed monitoring programme. This includes actions which could be taken if adverse effects were found.

Figure 7: **Documenting the monitoring data**					
What needs to be monitored (effect)?	What sort of information is required (indicator)?	Where can the information be obtained (sources of information)?	Are there any gaps in existing information and how can these be resolved?	When should remedial action be considered?	What remedial action could be taken?

Indicative list of plans and programmes subject to the SEA Directive

This is an indicative list of plans and programmes which are subject to the SEA Directive in some or all cases. It is not possible to give a definitive list because of the number of plans and programmes in existence and the varying extent to which the Directive's criteria apply, either to types of plan or programme or to individual plans or programmes within a type. The present list will be used in reporting to the European Commission on the implementation of the Directive.

LAND USE AND SPATIAL PLANNING

- Structure Plans

- Local Plans

- Unitary Development Plans

- Area Plans (Northern Ireland)

- Minerals Local Plans

- Minerals Plans (Scotland)

- Waste Local Plans

- Combined Minerals and Waste Local Plans

- Subject Local Plans (Scotland)

- The Mayor's Spatial Development Strategy (London)

Under the Planning and Compulsory Purchase Act 2004, the following plans in England and Wales are subject to Sustainability Appraisals which fully incorporate the requirements of the Directive:

- Local Development Documents, comprising Development Plan Documents and Supplementary Planning Documents

- Local Development Plans (Wales)

- Regional Spatial Strategies (these will take the form of a series of revisions to existing Regional Planning Guidance)

Other regional and local authority plans and programmes

The Directive will apply to all plans and programmes in most of the following categories. In certain cases, however, some individual plans and programmes will meet the Directive's criteria while others will not. To establish whether SEA is required, the authorities concerned should refer to the diagram of the criteria published by ODPM (See Appendix 1).

Regional Transport Strategies are to be produced as integral parts of English Regional Spatial Strategies, and are expected to be covered by the SEA of the RSS. Where there is a high degree of integration between other plans, the scope for integrated SEA should be explored.

- Regional Economic Strategies (Regional Development Agencies)

- Regional Development Strategy for Northern Ireland (and associated reviews)

- Regional Transport Strategies

- Review of Regional Transportation Strategy (Northern Ireland)

- Regional Housing Strategies

- Community Strategies (Appendix 2 of the ODPM Guidance for Planning Authorities on the Directive explains when the Directive will apply)

- Local Transport Plans

- Local Air Quality Action Plans

- Local Housing Strategies

- Recreation/Sports Strategies and Action Plans

- Primary Care Trusts Local Delivery Plans

Environmental protection and management

The Directive will apply to the following plans and programmes (in many cases case-by-case screening will be needed for significant environmental effects):

- Revisions to the Waste Strategy 2000

- River Basin Management Plans/Programmes of Measures

- Salmon Action Plans

Plans and programmes for industrial sectors

- Offshore Oil and Gas Licensing Rounds

- Offshore Windfarm Licensing Rounds

- Water Company Resource Plans

- Water Service Capital Works Programme (Northern Ireland)

Frequently Asked Questions on the SEA Directive

European Commission guidance on the SEA Directive ("Implementation of Directive 2001/42 on the Assessment of the Effects of Certain Plans and Programmes on the Environment") provides useful advice on interpreting many of the terms used in the Directive. It is available on the EU website http://europa.eu.int/comm/environment/eia/030923_sea_guidance.pdf.

HOW WILL THE DIRECTIVE BE TRANSPOSED INTO UK LAW?

The Directive is transposed by Regulations under the European Communities Act 1972. One set of Regulations covers all plans and programmes subject to the Directive which relate either solely to England or to both England and other parts of the UK. Separate Regulations for plans and programmes which relate solely to Scotland or Wales or Northern Ireland have been introduced by the Devolved Administrations in Scotland and Wales (the Scottish Executive and Welsh Assembly Government) and in Northern Ireland, the Department of Environment.

WHICH PLANS AND PROGRAMMES REQUIRE SEA UNDER THE DIRECTIVE?

The ODPM, Devolved Administrations and other bodies concerned have developed an indicative list, included in this Guide. This will be used for reporting purposes to the EU Commission and kept up to date.

HOW WILL A RESPONSIBLE AUTHORITY DECIDE WHETHER THE DIRECTIVE APPLIES TO A PLAN OR PROGRAMME?

A diagram showing how the Directive's criteria apply is at Appendix 1 of this Guide. In many cases the key question is whether a plan or programme has significant environmental effects; the Directive sets out basic criteria for the significance of effects in Annex II.

WHAT IS MEANT BY "SET THE FRAMEWORK FOR FUTURE DEVELOPMENT CONSENT OF PROJECTS" IN ARTICLES 3(2)(A) AND 3(4)?

The European Commission guidance suggests that this means the plan or programme contains criteria or conditions which guide the way the consenting authority decides an application for development consent. "Consent" here refers not only to formal planning consent but more broadly to all consents, permits, licences and other permissions necessary for the establishment of a new activity. Setting the framework is thus a matter of fact and degree.

WHAT SEA GUIDANCE IS AVAILABLE IN THE UK?

The SEA Practical Guide is intended to apply to all plans and programmes in the UK subject to the Directive. Specific guidance has, however, been developed for certain plans and programmes, particularly land use and spatial planning and transport planning. Readers should use the relevant specific guidance when preparing those types of plans and programmes.

HOW IS THE SIGNIFICANCE OF ENVIRONMENTAL EFFECTS ASSESSED?

This must be a matter for professional judgement. Annex II of the Directive provides a list of criteria that can be used to judge whether an environmental effect is significant. Further advice on interpretation of the criteria set out in Annex II is provided in the European Commission guidance on the SEA Directive

IF AN SEA HAS BEEN DONE, IS EIA STILL NEEDED?

The SEA Directive does not disapply the EIA Directive. In practice an SEA will typically be concerned with broad proposals and alternatives, while EIA is project-specific and requires more detailed information on the effects of a particular proposal on the environment. SEAs will help with the preparation of an EIA but will not remove the need for one.

IF AN SEA HAS BEEN DONE ON A HIGH LEVEL OR "PARENT" PLAN OR PROGRAMME, IS ONE REQUIRED FOR PLANS OR PROGRAMMES AT LOWER TIERS OR LATER STAGES?

The Directive provides for avoidance of duplication between plans or programmes in hierarchies. In practice the extent of assessment needed will often depend on the relationship between the plans or programmes concerned. "Lower level" plans and programmes are generally more detailed and locationally specific than those at higher tiers, and an SEA may therefore be needed to assess effects not previously covered in the necessary detail.

IF SEA IS CONDUCTED AS PART OF A WIDER ASSESSMENT, WILL A SEPARATE ENVIRONMENTAL REPORT BE NEEDED?

The European Commission guidance states that the Environmental Report can be included in a wider assessment of the effects of the plan or programme – for example, as part of a sustainability assessment which also covers social and economic effects. It is however desirable to show clearly that the Directive has been complied with, for example by signposting to enable the components that meet the requirements for the Environmental Report to be readily identified.

WHO WILL DO SEAS?

The Directive does not specify who should carry out SEA. The obligation to ensure that an SEA is done will normally lie with the Responsible Authority which produces the plan or programme, but the work may be done either by the authority's own staff or by others such as consultants, or a combination of the two.

WILL THE UK SET UP A BODY TO APPROVE OR REVIEW SEAS? HOW WILL THE QUALITY OF SEAS BE CONTROLLED?

The Government has no plans to create a dedicated body to carry out or oversee SEAs. In general, we believe the best approach is to integrate this role into the overall arrangements for oversight of plans or programmes. We are developing methods for quality assurance as part of a foundation of good practice.

EC Directives and other international instruments related to the SEA Directive

EC Directives

Environmental Impact Assessment Directive (85/337/EEC, amended by 97/11/EC)

Requires Environmental Impact Assessment (EIA) of specified types of projects.
http://europa.eu.int/comm/environment/eia/full-legal-text/85337.htm

The Habitats Directive (92/43/EEC on the conservation of natural habitats and of wild fauna and flora)

http://europa.eu.int/comm/environment/nature/habdir.htm

The Water Framework Directive (2000/60/EC)

http://europa.eu.int/comm/environment/water/water-framework/index_en.html

United Nations Economic Commission for Europe (UNECE)

Convention on Environmental Impact Assessment in a transboundary context (1991) (the Espoo Convention)

Requires countries which are Parties to the Convention to notify and consult each other on the likely environmental impacts of proposed trans-national projects in the categories listed.
http://www.unece.org/env/eia/documents/conventiontextenglish.pdf

Protocol on Strategic Environmental Assessment (2003)

A Protocol to the Espoo Convention with similar requirements to the SEA Directive.
http://www.unece.org/env/eia/documents/protocolenglish.pdf

Convention on access to information, public participation and access to justice in environmental matters (1999) (the Aarhus Convention)

http://www.unece.org/env/eia/documents/conventiontextenglish.pdf

Glossary

Consultation Bodies: Authorities which because of their environmental responsibilities are likely to be concerned by the effects of implementing plans and programmes and must be consulted at specified stages of the SEA. The Consultation Bodies, designated in the SEA Regulations, are:

- England: Countryside Agency, English Heritage, English Nature, and the Environment Agency.

- Northern Ireland: Department of the Environment

- Scotland: Historic Scotland, Scottish Natural Heritage, and the Scottish Environment Protection Agency. (Scottish Regulations use the term "Consultation Authorities").

- Wales: Cadw (Welsh Historic Monuments), Countryside Council for Wales, and the Environment Agency Wales.

Environmental Appraisal: A form of environmental assessment used in the UK (primarily for development plans) since the early 1990s, supported by "Environmental Appraisal of Development Plans: A Good Practice Guide" (DoE, 1993); more recently superseded by sustainability appraisal. Some aspects of environmental appraisal foreshadow the requirements of the SEA Directive.

Environmental Assessment: Generically, a method or procedure for predicting the effects on the environment of a proposal, either for an individual project or a higher-level "strategy" (a policy, plan or programme), with the aim of taking account of these effects in decision-making. The term "Environmental Impact Assessment" (EIA) is used, as in European Directive 337/85/EEC, for assessments of projects. In the SEA Directive, an environmental assessment means "the preparation of an environmental report, the carrying out of consultations, the taking into account of the environmental report and the results of the consultations in decision-making and the provision of information on the decision", in accordance with the Directive's requirements.

Environmental Report: Document required by the SEA Directive as part of an environmental assessment, which identifies, describes and evaluates the likely significant effects on the environment of implementing a plan or programme.

Indicator: A measure of variables over time, often used to measure achievement of objectives.

- **Output Indicator:** An indicator that measures the direct output of the plan or programme. These indicators measure progress in achieving plan or programme objectives, targets and policies.

- **Significant Effects Indicator:** An indicator that measures the significant effects of the plan or programme.

- **Contextual indicator:** An indicator that measures changes in the context within which a plan or programme is being prepared or implemented.

Mitigation: Used in this Guide to refer to measures to avoid, reduce or offset significant adverse effects on the environment.

Objective: A statement of what is intended, specifying the desired direction of change in trends.

Plan or Programme: For the purposes of this Guide, the term "plan or programme" covers any plans or programmes to which the Directive applies.

Responsible Authority: The organisation which prepares a plan or programme subject to the Directive and is responsible for the SEA.

Scoping: The process of deciding the scope and level of detail of an SEA, including the environmental effects and alternatives which need to be considered, the assessment methods to be used, and the structure and contents of the Environmental Report.

Screening: The process of deciding whether a plan or programme requires SEA. (Appendix 1 shows how the Directive's criteria apply to plans and programmes.)

Strategic Environmental Assessment (SEA): Generic term used to describe environmental assessment as applied to policies, plans and programmes. In this Guide, "SEA" is used to refer to the type of environmental assessment required under the SEA Directive.

SEA Directive: European Directive 2001/42/EC "on the assessment of the effects of certain plans and programmes on the environment".

SEA Regulations: The regulations transposing the SEA Directive into UK law, including the Devolved Administrations of Northern Ireland, Scotland, and Wales. The SEA Regulations include:

- *The Environmental Assessment of Plans and Programmes Regulations 2004;*

- *The Environmental Assessment of Plans and Programmes Regulations (Northern Ireland) 2004;*

- *The Environmental Assessment of Plans and Programmes (Scotland) Regulations 2004;* and

- *The Environmental Assessment of Plans and Programmes (Wales) Regulations 2004.*

Significant environmental effects: Effects on the environment which are significant in the context of a plan or programme. Criteria for assessing significance are set out in Annex II of the SEA Directive.

Sustainability appraisal: A form of assessment used in the UK, particularly for regional and local planning, since the 1990s. Considers social and economic effects as well as environmental ones, and appraises them in relation to the aims of sustainable development. Made mandatory for Local Development Documents and reviews of Regional Spatial Strategies under the Planning and Compulsory Purchase Act 2004, in a form which incorporates the requirements of the SEA Directive. New draft guidance on Sustainability Appraisal, incorporating the requirements of the SEA Directive, will be available for England in September.

Appendices

Appendix 1: Application of the SEA Directive to plans and programmes

This diagram is intended as a guide to the criteria for application of the Directive to plans and programmes (PPs). It has no legal status.

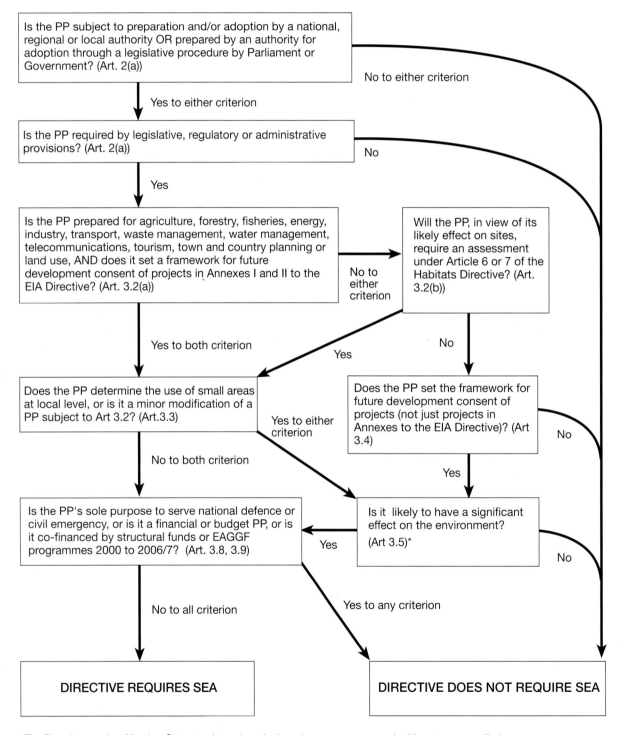

*The Directive requires Member States to determine whether plans or programmes in this category are likely to have significant environmental effects. These determinations may be made on a case by case basis and/or by specifying types of plan or programme.

Appendix 2: Other relevant plans, programmes and environmental protection objectives

The Environmental Report should provide information on the plan's or programme's relationship with other relevant plans and programmes and "the environmental protection objectives, established at international, [European] Community or national level, which are relevant to the plan ... and the way those objectives and any environmental considerations have been taken into account during its preparation" (Directive Annex I a, d).

No list of such plans, programmes or objectives can be definitive, but relevant plans and programmes may include:

- Land use or spatial plans for areas affected by the plan or programme, including those at different geographical levels (e.g. Regional Spatial Strategies, Local Development Frameworks and their component documents)

- Plans and programmes for specific sectors or types of activity, e.g., Regional Economic Strategies, Local Transport Plans, Minerals or Waste Development Plans

- European Directives, including the Habitats, Birds, Nitrates, Air Quality, Water Framework and Waste Framework Directives

- International undertakings such as those on greenhouse gases in the Kyoto Protocol

- UK initiatives such as Biodiversity Action Plans

- The UK Sustainable Development Strategy, and those of England, Wales, Scotland, and Northern Ireland

- White Papers setting out policies (e.g. Urban, Rural, Aviation)

- Planning Policy Statements and Minerals Planning Guidance

- Environmental management and resource plans, e.g. River Basin Management Plans, Water Resources Strategies

Appendix 3: Devising SEA objectives, indicators and targets

The Directive does not require objectives to be developed for the SEA itself, but they are widely used in SEA to ensure that the right level of consideration is achieved.

An objective is a statement of what is intended, specifying a desired direction of change. For this guidance, a distinction needs to be made between three types of objectives:

- *Plan objectives* are the objectives adopted for the plan in question, usually through a process of expert consideration, public consultation and political approval. Government guidance increasingly requires plan objectives to be based on sustainability considerations, and the development of SEA objectives may help to promote ideas for making them more environmentally friendly and sustainable.

- *External objectives* are other objectives to which planners must have regard independently from the SEA process. They include environmental protection objectives (which, if binding, must be covered in the Environmental Report), but they can also be economic or social, for instance a policy requirement to build a given number of houses.

- *SEA objectives* provide a methodological yardstick against which the environmental effects of the plan can be tested. These objectives are distinct from plan and external objectives, though they will often overlap with them. They may be "inherited" from the environmental protection objectives of Stage A, but may also include additional (often more locally focused) objectives.

Objectives can be expressed so that they are measurable (e.g. an objective to "reduce greenhouse gas emissions", could be expressed as "reduce CO_2 emissions by 12.5% by 2010"). The achievement of objectives is normally measured by using indicators.

SEA objectives can often be derived from environmental protection objectives identified in other plans and programmes or from a review of baseline information and environmental problems. The Consultation Bodies may also have suggestions for SEA objectives.

Figure 8 suggests some SEA objectives and indicators. They should be adapted to take account of local circumstances and concerns. For instance, local environmental objectives should be added to reflect local-level circumstances; objectives that are irrelevant to the area deleted; and more detailed objectives added. A plan concerned with minerals, for example, could include more objectives for soil and water quality, maintenance of the hydrological regime, and mineral reserves, and could express them in more detailed terms.

Figure 8: Examples of SEA objectives and indicators

SEA topics	possible SEA objectives (to be adapted to regional/local circumstances by deletions, additions and refinements)	possible SEA indicators: ways of quantifying the baseline, prediction, monitoring (to be adapted to regional/local circumstances by deletions, additions and refinements)
Biodiversity, fauna and flora	• avoid damage to designated wildlife sites and protected species • maintain biodiversity, avoiding irreversible losses • restore the full range of characteristic habitats and species to viable levels • reverse the long term decline in farmland birds • ensure the sustainable management of key wildlife sites and the ecological processes on which they depend • provide opportunities for people to come into contact with and appreciate wildlife and wild places	• reported levels of damage to designated sites • achievement of Biodiversity Action Plan targets • reported condition of nationally important wildlife sites • achievement of 'Accessible Natural Greenspace Standards' • number/area of Local Nature Reserves
Population and human health	• protect and enhance human health • reduce and prevent crime, reduce fear of crime • decrease noise and vibration	• size of population • changes in demography • years of healthy life expectancy • mortality by cause • recorded crimes per 1,000 population • fear of crime surveys • number of transport accidents • number of people affected by ambient noise levels • proportion of tranquil areas
Water and soil	• limit water pollution to levels that do not damage natural systems • maintain water abstraction, run-off and recharge within carrying capacity (including future capacity) • reduce contamination, and safeguard soil quality and quantity • minimize waste, then re-use or recover it through recycling, composting or energy • recovery • maintain and restore key ecological processes (e.g. hydrology, water quality, coastal processes)	• quality (biology and chemistry) of rivers, canals and freshwater bodies • quality and quantity of groundwater • water use (by sector, including leakage) and availability • water availability for water-dependent habitats, especially designated wetlands • amount/loss of greenfield/brownfield land • number of houses affected by subsidence, instability, etc. • housing density • waste disposed of in landfill • contaminated land
Air	• limit air pollution to levels that do not damage natural systems • reduce the need to travel	• number of days of air pollution • achievement of Emission Limit Values • population living in Air Quality Management Area • access to key services • distances travelled per person per year by mode of transport • modal split • traffic volumes
Climate Factors	• reduce greenhouse gas emissions • reduce vulnerability to the effects of climate change e.g. flooding, disruption to travel by extreme weather, etc.	• electricity and gas use • electricity generated from renewable energy sources and CHP located in the area • energy consumption per building and per occupant • CO emissions • flood risk

Cultural heritage and landscape	• preserve historic buildings, archaeological sites and other culturally important features • create places, spaces and buildings that work well, wear well and look well • protect and enhance the landscape everywhere and particularly in designated areas • value and protect diversity and local distinctiveness • improve the quantity and quality of publicly accessible open space Cultural heritage and landscape	• percentage of Listed Buildings and archaeological sites 'at risk' • number and proportion of vacant dwellings • building functionality: use, access, space • building impact: form and materials, internal environment, urban and social integration, character and innovation • percentage of land designated for particular quality or amenity value, including publicly accessible land and greenways • proportion of population within 200m of parks and open spaces

Responsible Authorities should bear the following considerations in mind at this stage:

- SEA objectives should focus on outcomes (or ends), not how the outcomes will be achieved ("inputs" or means). For example, they should focus on improved biodiversity, rather than protection of specific wildlife sites. This provides a cross-check on whether plan objectives, which are often framed in input terms, are the best possible ones for the environment.

- The development of SEA objectives and indicators and the collection of baseline information should inform each other. As the objectives become clearer, they should help to focus and restrict the collection of baseline information, whilst the baseline information should help to identify which SEA objectives are of most concern for a particular plan.

- Objectives should be linked to indicators explicitly measuring progress or otherwise towards them.

- Each objective should be genuinely needed and should not duplicate or overlap with other objectives. Experience suggests that between 12 and 25 objectives are normally enough to cover the range of topics needed for SEA and to keep the process efficient and manageable.

Existing objectives and indicators may be "inherited" from other plans or programmes. In such cases those carrying out the SEA should ensure that these objectives reflect the aims of the SEA Directive (see Chapter 2), i.e. they should be environmental objectives, not plan or programme objectives.

It may be useful to test the internal compatibility of the SEA objectives, for instance using a framework such as Figure 9. There may be tensions between objectives that cannot be resolved: the compatibility assessment should clarify these so that subsequent decisions are well based, and mitigation or alternatives can be considered.

Figure 9: **Testing compatibility of SEA objectives**					
SEA objective					
Objective 1					✔ compatible
Objective 2	✔				✗ incompatible
Objective 3	✔	✗			blank: no links
Objective 4	✗		✔		
Objective 5	✔	✔	✔		
	Obj've 1	Obj've 2	Obj've 3	Obj've 4	...

Some objectives may be more important than others. It may be worthwhile to give a rough ranking of objectives, or to highlight those which are judged to be particularly important – for instance because current conditions are problematic or because they are of particular concern to the public – to help focus the later stages of the SEA.

Appendix 4: Sources of baseline information

There are many sources of environmental information, but Responsible Authorities should always assess the value of any information in relation to its needs. An information set may not be appropriate for an authority's purpose; it may be unavailable at the right scale, out of date, unreliable, partial or biased. Where information is problematic, choices will need to be made on whether to avoid using it, make use of it with an explanation of its limitations, or collect further information to remove uncertainty. Information collection should focus on issues and scales relevant to the plan in question, to avoid the preparation of a generalised "State of the Environment" report.

The following tables list a selection of sources of information for describing the baseline environment in an SEA. The first section lists information sources that cover multiple topics. The second section lists sources that focus on specific SEA topics. The tables do not claim to be comprehensive. In particular, regional and county level monitoring sites are very useful sources of additional information.

The websites are correct as of June 2004.

Source of data	Examples of available datasets	Level
General		
Audit Commission and IDeA: Library of Local Performance Indicators www.local-pi-library.gov.uk www.audit-commission.gov.uk www.idea-knowledge.gov.uk	Includes a list of quality of life indicators.	
Defra www.defra.gov.uk www.defra.gov.uk/environment/statistics www.defra.gov.uk/environment/statistics/pubatt/download/pdf/survey2001.pdf www.defra.gov.uk/erdp/docs/regchapindex.htm	Quality of air, water, soil, public attitudes to the environment, regional statistics	Regional
The Environment and Heritage Service, Northern Ireland www.ehsni.gov.uk		
Environment Agency www.environment-agency.gov.uk/yourenv		
Countryside Agency www.countryside.gov.uk www.ccnetwork.org.uk	Designated areas and the landscape, landscape character assessment	Regional
Multi-Agency Geographic Information for the Countryside www.magic.gov.uk	Ward-level GIS information	Local
ODPM – Local Government Performance www.bvpi.gov.uk	Local authority actions and activities, mostly response indicators.	Local

Source of data	Examples of available datasets	Level
Sustainable Development The UK Government Approach: Achieving A Better Quality of Life www.sustainable-development.gov.uk www.sustainable-development.gov.uk/sustainable/quality99 www.sustainable-development.gov.uk/indicators/regional/2001	Wide range of quality of life data at local, regional and national levels.	National/Regional
Office for National Statistics (ONS) www.statistics.gov.uk www.neighbourhood.statistics.gov.uk	Population trends, social and economic data, public attitudes, etc.	Local
Regional Observatories and Information Partnerships, Intelligence Units www.regionalobservatories.org.uk East Midlands www.eastmidlandsobservatory.org.uk East of England www.eastofenglandobservatory.org.uk London www.london.gov.uk North East www.n-e-region.com North West www.nwriu.co.uk South East www.see-in.co.uk South West www.swro.info, www.swenvo.org.uk West Midlands www.wmro.org.uk Yorkshire and the Humber www.yorkshirefutures.com	Regional Observatories enable access to key regional data and intelligence. Working on a range of economic, social, and environmental issues, they do this by: • providing analysis of data and research • helping to disseminate and widen access to intelligence • conducting research to fill data gaps.	Local
County council and other regional and local monitoring sites (including Annual Monitoring Reports)		Local
Biodiversity, flora and fauna		
Association of Local Government Ecologists www.alge.org.uk		
British Butterfly Conservation Society www.butterfly-conservation.org	Butterflies.	National
British Society for Botanical Info. www.bsbi.org.uk	Flora.	National
British Trust for Ornithology www.bto.org	Bird trends.	National
Countryside Agency www.countryside.gov.uk	Countryside character, landscape etc.	Regional
Defra www.defra.gov.uk www.defra.gov.uk/environment/statistics	Air quality, inland water quality and use, waste and recycling, noise, land use and land cover, public attitudes to environment etc.	Regional
The National Heritage Directorate of Environment and Heritage Service www.ehsni.gov.uk/natural/natural.shtml		

Source of data	Examples of available datasets	Level
English Nature www.english-nature.org.uk	Designations, Local Authority managed SSSIs etc.	Local
Environment Agency www.environment-agency.gov.uk/yourenv	Environmental facts and figures, Environment Agency indicators (air, climate, land, people and lifestyles, pollution, resources and waste, water, wildlife) etc.	Local
Joint Nature Conservation Committee www.jncc.gov.uk	Site specific information e.g. Ramsar sites, wildlife and nature conservation, marine and coastal information.	National
Local Wildlife Trusts and Local Biological Record Centres		Local
National Biodiversity Network www.nbn.org.uk, www.searchnbn.net, www.ukbap.org.uk	A network of biodiversity and wildlife information.	National
Centre for Ecology and Hydrology www.ceh.ac.uk	Terrestrial and freshwater environmental research	Local
Plantlife www.plantlife.org.uk	Flora.	National
RSPB www.rspb.org.uk www.rspb.org.uk/science/birdweb	Bird monitoring and survey work.	Local
Water and soil		
British Geological Survey www.bgs.ac.uk	Minerals, unstable land, contaminated land, groundwater etc.	Local
Soil Resources Institute www.silsoe.cranfield.ac.uk/nsri	Sustainable management of soil and land resources	Local
Defra www.defra.gov.uk www.defra.gov.uk/environment/statistics	Air quality, inland water quality and use, waste and recycling, noise, land use and land cover, public attitudes to environment etc.	Regional
Environment Agency www.environment-agency.gov.uk/subjects/waste/315439	Water quality, floodplains, waste management, etc.	Local
The Environment and Heritage Service, Northern Ireland www.ehsni.gov.uk		
Centre for Ecology and Hydrology www.ceh.ac.uk	Terrestrial and freshwater environmental research	Local
DTI www.offshore-sea.org.uk	Off-shore oil and gas, renewable energy, marine issues	Local

Source of data	Examples of available datasets	Level
Air		
Department for Transport www.transtat.dft.gov.uk	Traffic levels, modal split, environmental impact	Regional
Defra www.airquality.co.uk/archive/laqm/laqm.php	Local Air Quality Management Plans	Local
Commission for Integrated Transport www.cfit.gov.uk/reports		National
The Environment and Heritage Service, Northern Ireland www.ehsni.gov.uk		
The Department for Regional Development, Northern Ireland www.drdni.gov.uk		
Climatic factors		
Defra www.airquality.co.uk	Local Air Quality Management Plans	Local
ODPM www.planning.odpm.gov.uk/lucs	Land use changes, flood risks	Regional
Renewable Energy Statistics Database www.restats.org.uk, www.etsu.com/RESTATS	Renewable energy sites, capacity and generation etc.	Regional
UK Climate Impacts Programme www.ukcip.org.uk	CO_2 emissions, climate change effects.	Regional
OFGEM www.ofgem.gov.uk/ofgem	CHP, energy providers	Regional
The Environment and Heritage Service, Northern Ireland www.ehsni.gov.uk		
Population and human health		
Defra www.defra.gov.uk/environment/noise	Noise.	Regional
Department for Transport www.transtat.dft.gov.uk	Traffic levels, accidents, modal split, etc.	Regional
Department of Health www.doh.gov.uk	Statistics and surveys of health levels and health care provision.	Local
Health and Safety Executive www.hse.gov.uk	Health in employment related statistics.	National
Health Development Agency Evidence Base www.hda-online.org.uk/evidence		
HealthPromis http://healthpromis.hda-online.org.uk	Evidence-based public health, health promotion and health inequalities.	
Home Office – Research and Statistics www.homeoffice.gov.uk/rds/index.htm	Crime, fear of crime statistics, patterns of criminality, etc.	Regional
Our Health Nation www.ohn.gov.uk		

Source of data	Examples of available datasets	Level
Public Health Electronic Library www.phel.gov.uk/		
Public Health Observatories www.pho.org.uk	Various public health and related statistics.	Local
Department of Health, Social Services and Public Safety, Northern Ireland www.dhsspsni.gov.uk		
Department for Regional Development, Northern Ireland www.drdni.gov.uk		
The Health and Safety Executive for Northern Ireland www.hseni.gov.uk		
Material assets		
ODPM www.housing.odpm.gov.uk/statistics/publicat	Housing completions, tenant satisfaction, etc.	Regional
Empty Homes Agency www.emptyhomes.com	Vacant properties	Regional
Cultural, heritage and landscape		
Countryside Agency www.countryside.gov.uk	State of the Countryside Reports and data, Countryside Indicator Research, landscape character, rural services survey etc.	Regional
English Heritage www.english-heritage.org.uk	State of the Historic Environment Report.	National
Local Authority Historic Environment Record Centres	Designated and non-designated sites.	Local
ODPM www.housing.odpm.gov.uk/factsheet/dwelling	Housing statistics, research and factsheets.	National
ODPM www.press.dtlr.gov.uk/pns/DisplayPN.cgi?pn_id=2000_0260	Green Belt	Local
The Built Heritage Directorate of Enviornment and Heritage Service www.ehsni.gov.uk/built/built.shtml		

Appendix 5: Collecting and presenting baseline information and trends

Sufficient information needs to be collected to identify the environmental issues and trends that characterise the areas affected by the plan or programme and to provide the evidence base against which its potential effects can be measured and assessed.

DECIDING WHAT INFORMATION TO COLLECT

The following principles can help to manage the collection of information:

- The information collected should be relevant and appropriate to the spatial scale of the plan or programme.

- The focus for information collection should be those aspects of the environmental character of the plan or programme area that are: (i) sufficient to identify the key environmental issues that are relevant to the plan or programme area; and (ii) aspects upon which the plan or programme may have a significant effect.

- The data and information collected should be relevant to the SEA objectives and indicators.

TYPES AND SOURCES OF BASELINE INFORMATION

Baseline information may be both quantitative or qualitative. Quantitative information sets are usually built up from existing monitoring and research activities while qualitative information is likely to be based on judgement. For the purposes of SEA qualitative information needs to be supported by reasoned evidence.

Responsible Authorities will probably already hold some of the environmental information they need, but there may be gaps in the information that need to be filled in order to provide an appropriate baseline for the SEA process. There are many different sources and forms of information, and so it is important to explore all avenues before deciding that new information needs to be collected. Some different sources of information include:

- Information included in other legislation, strategies, plans or programmes, which set the context for plan or programme preparation (see Appendix 2).

- Service providers (e.g. Consultation Bodies), who may be able to provide environmental data as well as technical advice and information.

- Other consultees, including both representative bodies and members of the public, who often have a wealth of knowledge and understanding of the strategy or plan area, e.g. local conservation groups

Not all information may be available immediately. The SEA team should consider whether improvements are needed to current information collection to fill existing gaps. Ways of improving the availability of information can be included in proposals for monitoring the implementation of the plan or programme.

MAPPING AND PRESENTATION OF INFORMATION

It is often useful to map information, to show how it varies across the plan or programme area. Using time data series, it is also possible to show how changes have occurred over time. Geographical Information Systems (GIS) are particularly useful in this respect. They enable layers of information to be built up, and it is possible to examine how closely one set of information relates to another. In this way, geographical patterns and linkages can begin to be established and explored. Where data cannot be mapped, the use of graphs, diagrams and other visual forms of representation can help to make the data easier to understand.

IDENTIFYING TRENDS

Much information will record the state of the environment at a point or points in time – providing a historic record or a snapshot in time. Where possible, however, it will be important to examine trends, both historical trends and likely future trends given continuation of existing policies, plans and programmes under a "do minimum" or "business as usual" scenario. There should be agreement about what these scenarios are. "Do minimum" might mean no further development in an area, while "business as usual" often means a continuation of the current plan or programme. In particular, it will be useful to examine whether trends demonstrate that existing plans and programmes are achieving agreed targets or moving towards or away from targets. This trend analysis should help to highlight existing and potential future environmental problems.

PRESENTING BASELINE INFORMATION

Figure 10 gives an example of how baseline information can be organised and presented.

Figure 10: **Possible way of organising and presenting baseline information**					
SEA Topic	Indicator	Quantified information (for Responsible Authority unless otherwise noted) [figures in brackets = information sources]	Comparators and targets	Trend	Issues/ constraints
POPULATION AND HUMAN HEALTH	% of people in authority's area describing their health as not good	5.8% [25] 2001	England and Wales 9.2% [25] 2001	6.4% in 1999: getting better	Favourable situation. Lower than national average and getting better.
	Proportion of population not getting minimum level of healthy exercise	10% of people exercise 3 or more times a week. [3] 1999/2000	This is the lowest rate for any district in the region. [3] 1999/2000	No trend available	Unfavourable situation – low level of exercise.
	No. people affected by ambient noise			No trend available	Unable to identify situation
	Public concern over noise	Noise is not perceived to be a problem. [5] 2003		No trend available	Favourable situation

Appendix 6: Assessing secondary, cumulative and synergistic effects

INTRODUCTION

Many environmental problems result from the accumulation of multiple small and often indirect effects, rather than a few large and obvious ones. Examples include loss of tranquillity, changes in the landscape, loss of heathland and wetland, and climate change. These effects are very hard to deal with on a project-by-project basis through Environmental Impact Assessment. It is at the SEA level that they are most effectively identified and addressed.

Annex I of the SEA Directive requires that the assessment of effects should include secondary, cumulative and synergistic effects.

Secondary or indirect effects are effects that are not a direct result of the plan, but occur away from the original effect or as a result of a complex pathway. Examples of secondary effects are a development that changes a water table and thus affects the ecology of a nearby wetland; and construction of one project that facilitates or attracts other developments.

Cumulative effects arise, for instance, where several developments each have insignificant effects but together have a significant effect; or where several individual effects of the plan (e.g. noise, dust and visual) have a combined effect.

Synergistic effects interact to produce a total effect greater than the sum of the individual effects. Synergistic effects often happen as habitats, resources or human communities get close to capacity. For instance a wildlife habitat can become progressively fragmented with limited effects on a particular species until the last fragmentation makes the areas too small to support the species at all.

These terms are not mutually exclusive. Often the term cumulative effects is taken to include secondary and synergistic effects.

PRINCIPLES OF ASSESSING CUMULATIVE EFFECTS

- Cumulative effects should be considered throughout, and as part of the SEA and plan and programme preparation, not as a separate process

- Assessing cumulative effects should be focused on identifying the total effect of both direct and indirect effects on receptors. Receptors may include natural resources (e.g. air, water, soil), sections of the population (e.g. people living in particular areas or vulnerable members of the community) or ecosystems and species (e.g. heathland).

- Cumulative effects need to be considered in relation to the nature and extent of the receptors, such as ecosystems and communities, rather than administrative boundaries.

- The cumulative effects of policies and proposals within a plan or programme and those which may result from interaction with the effects of other plans and programmes should be considered

- In considering cumulative effects, how close the plan or programme, in association with other past, present and likely future actions, will bring the receptors to their capacity/threshold to remain productive or sustainable should be assessed.

- Identifying cumulative effects involves considerable uncertainty. If it is not feasible to eliminate this, the uncertainty should be documented.

ASSESSING CUMULATIVE EFFECTS AS PART OF SEA

Figure 11 sets out key points in the assessment of cumulative, secondary and synergistic effects during the SEA process.

Figure 11: Key stages of SEA and the consideration of cumulative, secondary and synergistic effects	
Key Stages of Sustainability Appraisal	Key points in the assessment of cumulative, secondary and synergistic effects
Stage A: Setting the context and establishing the baseline	**Identifying other relevant plans or programmes and environmental protection objectives** • Identify key receptors which may be subject to cumulative effects • Consider any cumulative effects that other current and reasonably foreseeable plans, programmes and strategies may have on key receptors. Some plans may be more influential than others: this should be noted. **Collecting baseline information** • For each key receptor document: – The current status – How this has changed over time, and how it is likely to change in the future without the implementation of the plan or programme – What has led to the present condition – How close to capacity the key receptor is, that is, can it absorb further effects before changes become significant and/or irreversible • Recognise that the scope of cumulative effects can be very wide and that it is important to focus the assessment. • Baseline for cumulative effects may be summarised in a format similar to Figure 10. **Identifying environmental problems** • Identify receptors that are particularly sensitive, in decline or are near their threshold (since these components may not be able to cope with the multiple stresses). **Developing SEA objectives** • Development of SEA objectives, indicators and targets should be influenced by significant cumulative effects identified and environmental thresholds/capacity.
Stage B: Deciding the scope of SEA and developing strategic alternatives	**Testing the plan or programme objectives against the SEA objectives** • Testing the consistency between plan or programme objectives and SEA objectives may help highlight potential cumulative effects. **Appraising strategic alternatives** • Ensure that the different alternatives that are selected for testing as part of the assessment are also assessed for their cumulative, secondary or synergistic effects. • Recognise that the assessment of cumulative, secondary or synergistic effects of different alternatives could be used to screen out unacceptable alternatives. **Consulting on the scope of SEA** • Set out the likely significant cumulative effects of the preferred strategic alternatives and plan to consider cumulative effects as part of the rest of the SEA process.

Key Stages of Sustainability Appraisal	Key points in the assessment of cumulative, secondary and synergistic effects
Stage C: Assessing the effects of the plan or programme	**Predicting the effects of the plan or programme including alternatives** • Predict and assess the cumulative effects of the plan or programme on the key receptors, i.e. the cumulative effects of current and reasonably foreseeable plans, programmes and strategies, with and without the plan or programme. • Recognise that there is uncertainty in predicting effects and determining significance and this can arise due to the variation in natural systems and their interactions; a lack of information, knowledge or scientific agreement regarding cause-effect relationship; or the inability of predictive models to accurately represent complex systems. • Accept that the level of risk and uncertainty associated with cumulative effects increases at the higher planning levels because scales are broader and issues are generally larger. • Document limitations and inadequacies of data/information. • Recognise that there may be several approaches available to assist in the prediction of cumulative effects, and that there is not a single approach applicable to all situations. **Evaluating the effects of the plan or programme including alternatives** • Assessment should be both in terms of magnitude – the difference between the with and without plan or programme scenarios, and in terms of the capacity/threshold of the valuable environmental resources. **Mitigating adverse effects** • Document the measures envisaged to avoid, mitigate and negate cumulative effects. **Proposing measures to monitor the environmental effects of plan or programme implementation** • Document measures proposed to monitor significant cumulative effects recognising that it may be difficult to determine what 'share' of cumulative effects is due to the given plan or programme. **Preparing the Environmental Report** • Report cumulative effects in a transparent and accessible way and explain how they were identified and assessed. • Provide a description of how effects are assessed and which methods were adopted. • Provide a description of how the various forms of cumulative effects are most likely to occur in the plan or programme. • Describe the significant cumulative effects of the plan or programme on each receptor, recording assumptions and uncertainty.
Stage D: Consulting and decision-making	**Consulting on the draft plan or programme and the Environment Report** • Use the consultation process to help to predict and evaluate the cumulative effects of the plan or programme. **Assessment of significant changes** • Where significant changes are made to the plan or programme identify changes in the cumulative effects **Decision making and provision of information** • Provide information on how the cumulative effects, along with other significant effects of the plan or programme, were taken into account in preparing the plan or programme
Stage E: Monitoring implementation of the plan or programme	**Developing aims and methods for monitoring** • Monitoring should be carried out using the appropriate indicators which take account of cumulative effects as well as direct effects. **Responding to adverse effects** • It may be necessary to take action where significant adverse cumulative effects are identified as a result of monitoring.

METHODS FOR ASSESSING CUMULATIVE EFFECTS

Figure 12 identifies some of the various techniques that may be used in assessing cumulative effects, along with their advantages and disadvantages. It is for the practitioner undertaking the appraisal to choose which method is most appropriate. This may involve the use of various approaches that can be adapted and combine to suit particular needs rather than a single method. When selecting techniques consider:

- ability to organise, analyse and present information

- stage of the assessment (e.g. scoping, baseline data collection, analysis, reporting)

- types of issues involved and cumulative effects being examined

- key receptors being examined

- quality and extent of baseline data

- level of expertise available

Figure 12: Techniques for assessing cumulative, secondary and synergistic effects

Method	Description	Advantages	Disadvantages
Questionnaires, interviews and panels	Useful in gathering the wide range of information on multiple actions and receptors needed to address cumulative effects. Brainstorming sessions, interviews with knowledgeable individuals and group consensus building activities can help identify the important cumulative effects in the area.	Flexible and able to deal with subjective information	Cannot quantify effects and comparison of alternatives is subjective
Checklists	Identify potential cumulative effects by providing lists of common or likely effects and juxtaposing multiple actions and resources. This can be seen as a shortcut to scoping.	Systematic and concise	Can be inflexible and do not address interactions or cause-effect relationships
Matrices	Matrices use a tabular format to organise the interactions between human activities and resources of concern (see Figures 16 and 17).	Provides good visual summary and can be used to identify and evaluate effects to some degree	Can be complex and cumbersome and do not address cause-effect relationships
Causal Chain/ Network/ Systems analysis	Helps to identify the cause-effect relationships resulting in cumulative effects using flow diagrams. Allows the user to analyse the multiple effects of various actions and trace indirect effects on resources that accumulate from direct effects on other resources (see Figure 18).	Facilitate conceptualisation of cause-effect relationships and identify direct effects	No spatial or temporal scale and diagrams can be complex and cumbersome

Method	Description	Advantages	Disadvantages
Modelling	An analytical tool which enables the quantification of cause-effect relations which result in cumulative effects by simulation of environmental conditions.	Addresses cause-effect relationships and gives quantified results. Geographic boundaries and time-frames are usually explicit.	Needs a lot of time and data and extrapolation is still largely subjective. Can be difficult to adapt some models to a particular situation.
Trends analysis	Assesses the status of a resource, ecosystem or human community over time and usually results in graphical projection of past or future conditions. Changes in the occurrence or intensity of stressors over the same time period can also be determined. Trends can help the analyst identify cumulative effects, establish appropriate environmental baselines or project future cumulative effects.	Addresses accumulation over time and helps to identify problems	Needs a lot of data and extrapolation is still largely subjective
Overlay mapping and GIS	Used to identify where effects may occur. Can superimpose effects on receptors or resources to establish where effects may be significant	Flexible and easy to update. Can consider multiple projects and past, present and future options. Allows clear visual presentation.	Can be expensive and time consuming and difficult to quantify effects
Expert Opinion	A way of identifying and assessing effects. Expert panels can be formed to facilitate exchange of information and to express views on cumulative effects.	Particularly useful where other methods are not available but significant cumulative effects are considered likely	Relies on experts – may affect transparency or acceptance of the assessment process
Carrying Capacity & Threshold Analysis	Based in recognition that thresholds exist in the environment and that cumulative effects can result in thresholds being exceeded.	Useful in addressing accumulation of effects against thresholds and considering trends in the environment	It is not always possible to establish the threshold or carrying capacity for a particular resource or receptor

Figure 13: **Example of a table for recording cumulative effects and their causes**		
Cumulative Effect	Affected Receptor	Causes
Habitat fragmentation	Wildlife habitats	Use of land for flood management, transport infrastructure and industrial development
Climate change	Worldwide	Greenhouse gas emissions from industrial development and increases in traffic volumes
Loss of tranquillity	Countryside	Industrial development and increases in traffic volumes

Figure 14: **Example of a table for recording the cumulative effects of plan or programme on receptors**			
Policy no.	Effects on valued		
	Habitat fragmentation	Climate Change	Loss of tranquillity
New industry	0 (on brownfield sites)	- (additional trips)	0 (on existing brownfield sites)
Promote green technology industry	0 (on brownfield sites)	0 (no emissions)	0 (on existing brownfield sites)
Jobs close to home	0 (on brownfield sites)	+ (reduce travel distances)	0 (on existing brownfield sites)
Cumulative Effects	0	+	0
Commentary		Generally positive	

Further information is given in the European Commission's *Guidelines for the Assessment of Indirect and Cumulative Impacts as well as Impact Interactions* and the Canadian Environmental Assessment Agency's *Addressing Cumulative Environmental Effects* – see "References and further information" for details and links.

Appendix 7: Identifying and comparing alternatives

Alternatives may be described as the range of rational choices open to plan and programme-makers for delivering the plan or programme objectives. This guidance assumes that the SEA Directive's term "alternatives" is normally synonymous with "options" in plan and programme-making.

Assessment always involves comparison. The effects of a plan or programme can only be understood by comparing it with a state, an alternative or an objective. Alternatives should be compared with each other and with "business as usual" and/or "do nothing" options. These alternatives can then be compared with the predicted implementation of the current or existing plan, to show what would happen without the new plan or programme. A comparison of this can then be made with current environmental conditions to show which alternatives would improve or worsen current conditions. There is no one "correct" comparison: different comparisons will reveal different points, and more than one may be significant.

IDENTIFYING ALTERNATIVES

Alternatives put forward should be reasonable, realistic and relevant. Alternatives should also be sufficiently distinct in order to highlight the different environmental implications of each, so that meaningful comparisons can be made at a strategic level.

Some alternatives are discrete. These involve a choice between one alternative and another, as in Figure 15. These are often the broad options considered early in plan and programme preparation. Other alternatives can be combined in various ways. Plan or programme policies are often alternatives of this type. Alternatives may be grouped into scenarios, for instance rapid economic growth, "most sustainable" option, etc.

Figure 15: **Example of discrete alternatives**

An analysis of higher-level strategies identified three dimensions related to the provision of new housing as part of a wider exercise to stem population loss:

- The number of new houses needed to create sustainable neighbourhoods and attract households back

- The density of housing, which has a bearing on house type and design and is a key determinant of what prospective occupiers might find attractive

- The location of housing: in simplistic terms, greenfield v. brownfield.

Eight alternatives representing various combinations of these dimensions were identified:

1. Do the minimum: Little or no net new development – new build as replacement for demolition, only modest increases in dwellings through conversion of existing buildings, reduction in vacant properties and land, and more intensive use of buildings. De-allocate all existing greenfield allocations and no windfall developments beyond those already with permission.

2. No change: Maintain existing densities and greenfield allocations and allow development on windfall sites. Modest net increase in housing stock.

3. Meet target of 200 net new dwellings per year through option 1, plus density increase on cleared sites and development on previously developed land not used as open space. De-allocate all existing greenfield allocations.

4. Meet the RPG target through option 1, plus lower density increase than option 2, by retaining existing greenfield allocations.

5. Meet the RPG target through option 1, plus lower density increase than option 3, and increasing density on existing greenfield allocations, seeking up to a maximum 25% of development on greenfield sites.

6. Meet the regeneration strategy target (about 500 net new dwellings per year) through option 3, but with much higher densities.

7. Meet the regeneration strategy target through option 4, but with higher densities.

8. Meet the regeneration strategy target through option 5, with new greenfield allocations.

Clearly there could be many other targets between 200 and 500 net new dwellings per year.

For key plan or programme issues, a hierarchy of options should be considered, as shown at Figure 16. Obviation of demand is often environmentally and socially better than providing for demand or rationing consumption through price or limited capacity. For example, better local amenities or services might make some journeys unnecessary; and insulation and design standards can reduce the need for domestic heating. Obviation is not the same thing as restricting or thwarting demands which may simply lead to the displacement of a problem: it should be seen as looking for different, more sustainable, means to achieve human quality of life ends.

Figure 16: 'Hierarchy' of alternatives

need or demand: is it necessary?
Can the need or demand be met without implementing the plan or programme at all?
Can the proposal (development, infrastructure etc) be obviated?

mode or process: how should it be done?
Are there technologies or methods that can meet the need with less environmental damage than 'obvious' or traditional methods?

location: where should it go?

timing and detailed implementation:
When, in what form and in what sequence, should developments be carried out?
What details matter, and what requirements should be made about them?

To keep the big issues clear, the alternatives considered at this early stage should not be elaborated in too much detail. Only the main differences between the alternatives need to be considered and documented.

Figure 17 gives examples of alternatives which could fall under each of these headings.

Figure 17: Examples of alternatives

Topic	Obviation	Mode/type	Location	Implementation/ timing
Transport/ accessibility	Reduce the need to travel by locating amenities/ services nearer their users, or housing users nearer the amenities they need; helping people meet more needs at home (e.g. homeworking, information technology)	Encourage walking and cycling Support good public transport, matched to journey desires (e.g. provide sites for modal interchange, protect rail corridors)	Locate amenities and services together, so people can accomplish several errands in one trip, e.g. multi-functional town centres Locate bike stands and bus stops more conveniently than parking	Have walking/cycling infrastructure and public transport services in place before development comes in to use If extra traffic capacity is unavoidable, design at minimum necessary capacity, avoid discouraging other modes (e.g. design in traffic calming, safe routes for pedestrians and cyclists), minimise noise, land take and visual intrusion.

Topic	Obviation	Mode/type	Location	Implementation/timing
Housing	Match supply needs: • Encourage adaptation of buildings to maximise the potential for comfortable occupation (e.g. loft and garage conversions, subdivision of large houses) • High standard sheltered accommodation for older people as an alternative to staying in unnecessarily large houses Make best use of existing building stock: • Encourage living above shops • Conversion of redundant non-domestic buildings, loft conversions, flexible subletting of surplus space	Encourage walking and cycling Make best use of land: • Encourage infill, development of small sites, rebuilding at higher densities • Promote dense and land-efficient built forms, e.g. terraces, low rise flats, communal open spaces • Maximise density • Use existing infrastructure in new	Minimise new infrastructure demands (e.g. by avoiding locations remote from amenities) Focus new housing on brownfield sites and away from floodplains	Match timing of housing development to needs and to public service provision
Waste	Encourage developers to prepare waste management plans	Ensure that waste can be used as a resource by providing facilities for storing recyclable products (e.g. architectural salvage yards, sites for storage of recycled aggregates)	Locate waste management sites near source of waste and/or users of waste as resource	Provide recycling facilities at housing and employment sites Use materials efficiently in construction. Use recycled materials in construction.
Energy	Reduce demand for energy in housing by promoting low energy lighting and appliances, very efficient boilers, high insulation standards, conservatories and lobbies, large south-facing and small north-facing windows etc	Promote renewable energy, energy from waste, Combined Heat and Power	Small-Scale, community-owned renewable energy installations to minimise transmission loss.	Use best available energy effciency technologies in building construction and operation; site housing to optimise solar gain; use materials with low embodied energy
Water	Promote rainwater collection systems, effluent recycling	Consider several small facilities rather than one large one	Promote use of water-saving devices e.g. low-flow showers, low-flush toilets	Promote landscaping using plants that do not require much watering

Clearly not all of these options are applicable in all cases. For instance, demand reduction measures are often outside the control of the Responsible Authority. Some alternatives may not be practical, or within a Responsible Authority's powers, while others may not be appropriate to a particular stage or level of plan or programme. A wider range of alternatives will be available at a regional level than at a local level, and decisions made at the "higher" level will close off some alternatives. Nevertheless, "up the hierarchy" thinking could suggest a wider, and more sustainable, range of alternatives than hitherto considered.

Stakeholders may usefully be involved in the generation and assessment of both strategic and more detailed alternatives through consultation. Demonstrating that there are choices to be made is an effective way of engaging stakeholders in the process. The alternatives considered throughout the process should be documented and reasons given to why they are or are not taken forward.

ASSESSING ALTERNATIVES

The assessment of alternatives may be made in broad terms against the SEA objectives. This assessment must be in sufficient detail to identify the significant environmental effects of each alternative, highlighting where appropriate any cumulative, secondary and synergistic, short, medium, and long-term effects, and whether they are permanent or temporary.

When assessing alternatives, it may be helpful to consider:

- Are the alternatives distinct and clearly presented?

- Are they likely to have any adverse effects? Can these be reduced, avoided, or offset?

- Can positive effects be enhanced?

- Can any of the effects be quantified in a meaningful way?

- Who are likely to be the "winners", and "losers" for each alternative (e.g. rural versus urban dwellers; young versus old; people with cars versus those without; future versus current generations, etc)?

- Are any effects of the alternatives unclear or ambiguous? Is any further analysis appropriate?

- Are the effects likely to be variable over the short, medium and long-term?

As an input to a decision about preferred alternatives, it may be useful to summarise the assessment results for the different alternatives in one table (e.g. Figure 18 or Figure 19). This can help to identify the most sustainable alternative overall, or different alternatives that promote different aspects of sustainability. It can also suggest new, more sustainable, alternatives composed of different aspects of the initial alternatives. Symbols or other ways of presenting information regarding the likely effects (e.g. positive, negative, uncertain, not significant) can be used , but should always to accompanied by a commentary explaining and justifying the choice of symbol with reference to the baseline situation relevant to the sustainability objective. This helps promote transparency and aids users of the appraisal and secondly provides an opportunity to record opportunities for enhancement or mitigation.

Figure 19: **Example of comparison of alternatives [Need non-land use example]**									

Scale: + positive, – negative, +/- range of positive and negative effects

	Option 1: multi-function waste treatment facilities (management, storage and processing) in each population centre with >25,000 inhabitants				Option 2: limited function waste treatment facilities (management, recycling, and some treatment) dotted around the county provided on a basis of one facility per 10,000 inhabitants			
SEA/SA Objective	Short term	Med term	Long term	Comments/ explanation	Short term	Med term	Long term	Comments/ explanation
Limit air pollution to levels that do not damage natural systems	+/-	+/-	+/-	Operating conditions may reduce amount of pollution from waste treatment, but more vehicle trips needed to bring waste to the limited number of sites	+	++	+++	Easier access to treatment facilities should reduce the number and length of trips to assemble waste at the site. Effect is cumulative
Reduce the need to travel		+/-	–	Limited number of treatment sites results in more and longer trips. Effect accumulates as the volume of waste produced per capita rises	+	++	+++	As above
Preserve historic buildings, and other culturally important features				Has no obvious impact	–	–	–	Potential impact if new treatment sites affect valued or protected localities or sites. Unquantifiable at present

Figure 20: **Example table for assessment of alternatives against SEA objectives**				
SEA Objective	Option A		Option B	
	Performance	Commentary/ explanation	Performance	Commentary/ explanation
SEA Objective 1				
SEA Objective 2				
SEA Objective 3				
SEA Objective 4				
SEA Objective 5				
SEA Objective 6				
SEA Objective 7				
etc				
Additional Comments (including changes to the alternative) and Preferred Option				

Key for performance:
+ positive – negative O neutral ? uncertain
+ minor ++ major
A distinction could also be made between short, medium and long term, if appropriate

Appendix 8: Prediction and evaluation of effects

The most familiar form of SEA prediction and evaluation technique is a table such as that at Figure 5. Effects predictions are generally broad-brush and qualitative, e.g.

... getting worse over the next 15 years; or
... mildly negative, on a scale from strongly positive (++) to strongly negative (- -); or
... worse under Scenario A than under Scenario B

But the predictions could also be more detailed and quantitative, e.g. a measurable effect would

... increase from 10 to 12 parts per million between 2005 and 2020; or
... increase by 20% between 2005 and 2020; or
... increase by 20% by 2020 under Scenario A and by 16% under Scenario B; or
... exceed national standards by 6% by 2020.

In considering the effects of a plan or programme, some useful rules of thumb may be:

- When using symbols or other ways of presenting information regarding the likely effects (e.g. positive, negative, uncertain, not significant), always explain and justify the choice of symbol with reference to the baseline situation relevant to the SEA objective.

- Concentrate on the effects of the plan or programme, rather than other factors that may influence the achievement of the SEA objective – it is the influence of the plan or programme that is being assessed.

- Consider only effects that are likely to result from the influence of the plan or programme – discount those changes which would have happened anyway, irrespective of the plan or programme.

- Consider whether the effect is likely to be permanent or temporary, and the timescale over which the effect is likely to be observed.

- Provide detailed and quantitative predictions where possible but avoid using spurious measurements, not grounded in evidence.

- Consider the effects of displacement of environmental problems to other areas as a result of the plan or programme.

- If there are risks or uncertainties attached to the assessment, these should be clearly stated.

- Use the measurement of effects to improve the environmental performance of individual policies as well as the plan or programme as a whole.

Figure 21 suggests possible prediction and evaluation techniques and sources of further information.

Figure 22 gives a fuller explanation of issues to consider when filling in Figure 5. Following this flowchart helps to ensure that prediction, evaluation and mitigation are linked and that a full range of mitigation measures are considered.

Figure 21: **Prediction and evaluation techniques for SEA**						
Technique	SEA stage					Examples or sources of further information (see References for details of publications)
	describe baseline	identify impacts	predict impacts	evaluate impacts	ensure coherence	
Expert judgement	✓	✓	✓	✓	✓	
Public participation	✓	✓		✓		Audit Commission (2000)
Quality of Life Capital	✓			✓		Countryside Agency et al (2001)
Geographical information systems	✓		✓	✓		European Environment Agency (1998)
Network analysis		✓	✓			Figure A7.2
Modelling	✓		✓			European Commission (1999)
Scenario/sensitivity analysis			✓			
Multi-criteria analysis				✓		DETR (2001)
Carrying capacity, ecological footprints				✓		Chambers et al. (2000) European Commission (1999)
Compatibility assessment					✓	Figure 10

Figure 22: **The process of assessing the effects of a plan**

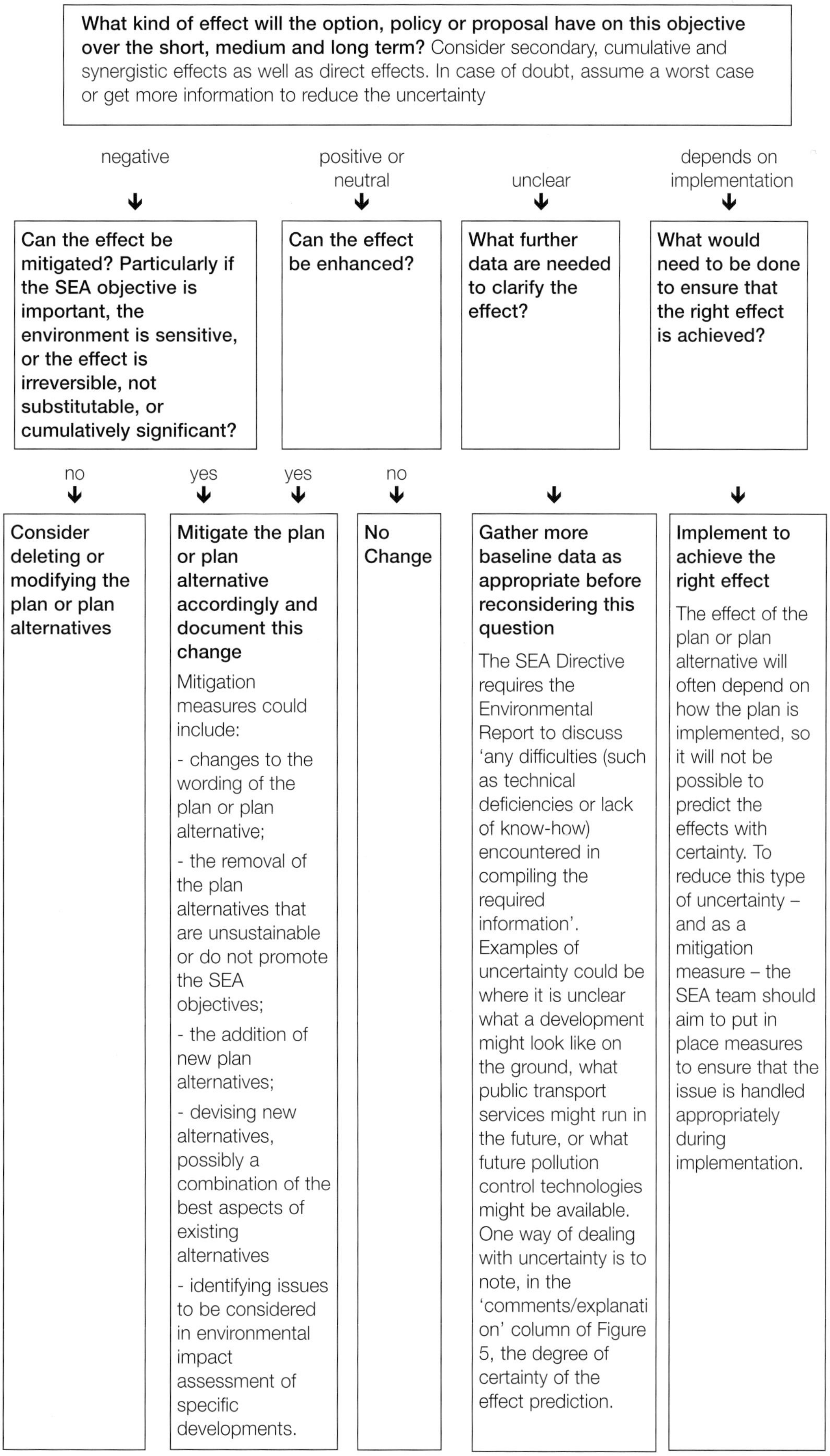

What kind of effect will the option, policy or proposal have on this objective over the short, medium and long term? Consider secondary, cumulative and synergistic effects as well as direct effects. In case of doubt, assume a worst case or get more information to reduce the uncertainty

negative	positive or neutral	unclear	depends on implementation

Can the effect be mitigated? Particularly if the SEA objective is important, the environment is sensitive, or the effect is irreversible, not substitutable, or cumulatively significant?	Can the effect be enhanced?	What further data are needed to clarify the effect?	What would need to be done to ensure that the right effect is achieved?

no	yes	yes	no		

Consider deleting or modifying the plan or plan alternatives	Mitigate the plan or plan alternative accordingly and document this change	No Change		Gather more baseline data as appropriate before reconsidering this question	Implement to achieve the right effect

Mitigate the plan or plan alternative accordingly and document this change

Mitigation measures could include:

- changes to the wording of the plan or plan alternative;

- the removal of the plan alternatives that are unsustainable or do not promote the SEA objectives;

- the addition of new plan alternatives;

- devising new alternatives, possibly a combination of the best aspects of existing alternatives

- identifying issues to be considered in environmental impact assessment of specific developments.

Gather more baseline data as appropriate before reconsidering this question

The SEA Directive requires the Environmental Report to discuss 'any difficulties (such as technical deficiencies or lack of know-how) encountered in compiling the required information'. Examples of uncertainty could be where it is unclear what a development might look like on the ground, what public transport services might run in the future, or what future pollution control technologies might be available. One way of dealing with uncertainty is to note, in the 'comments/explanation' column of Figure 5, the degree of certainty of the effect prediction.

Implement to achieve the right effect

The effect of the plan or plan alternative will often depend on how the plan is implemented, so it will not be possible to predict the effects with certainty. To reduce this type of uncertainty – and as a mitigation measure – the SEA team should aim to put in place measures to ensure that the issue is handled appropriately during implementation.

Appendix 9: Monitoring

INTRODUCTION

The Directive requires the significant environmental effects of implementing the plan or programme to be monitored to identify unforeseen adverse effects and to enable remedial action to be taken. Responsible Authorities may already be monitoring implementation of plans or programmes against their objectives or targets. Some of these may be environmental, but this will not necessarily be enough to satisfy the Directive; Responsible Authorities should ensure when designing their monitoring arrangements that they comply with this provision. For convenience, this guidance will use the term "SEA monitoring" to cover the overall monitoring of environmental effects.

SEA monitoring can be used to answer questions such as:

- Were the assessment's predictions of environmental effects accurate?

- Is the plan or programme contributing to the achievement of desired environmental objectives and targets?

- Are mitigation measures performing as well as expected?

- Are there any adverse environmental effects? Are these within acceptable limits, or is remedial action desirable?

Proposed monitoring framework

The SEA Directive does not specify that monitoring of significant environmental effects has to be done for each plan or programme individually. Nor does it need to be done directly by the Responsible Authority. Monitoring may cover several plans or programmes as long as sufficient information about environmental effects is provided for the individual plans or programmes. There is in other words scope for authority-wide monitoring, providing this can be done in such a way that the requirements of the Directive are met. The appropriate level at which to monitor depends on the type and scale of the plan or programme to be monitored.

A step-by-step guide for how a Responsible Authority may develop a monitoring system for plans and programmes is provided below.

Step 1: What needs to be monitored?

The first step is to consider exactly what needs to be monitored. Monitoring measures must be clearly linked to the SEA process, for example consider:

- The objectives, targets and indicators that were developed for the SEA (see Stage A of this guidance).

- Features of the environmental baseline that will indicate the effects of the plan (see Stage A).

- The likely significant effects that were identified during the effects assessment (see Stages B and C).

- The mitigation measures that were proposed to offset or reduce significant adverse effects (see Stage C).

Monitoring should consider both positive and negative effects.

Effects relate to the plan as a whole and monitoring should including consideration of cumulative, secondary and synergistic effects over and above the effects of the individual measures in the plan or programme, and effects over the lifespan of the plan.

It is not necessary to monitor everything or monitor an effect indefinitely. Instead monitoring should be focussed on:

- Significant environmental effects that may give rise to irreversible damage, with a view to identifying trends before such damage is caused.

- Significant effects where there was uncertainty in the SEA and where monitoring would enable preventative or mitigation measures to be taken.

Step 2: What sort of information is required?

The type (e.g. quantitative or qualitative) and the level of detail of environmental monitoring information required will depend on the characteristics and level of detail of the plan and its forecasted environmental effects.

SEA monitoring should involve measuring indicators which enable us to establish a causal link between implementation of the plan or programme and the likely significant effect being monitored. The monitoring framework should be established in a way that seeks to take account of external factors and focus upon the links between the plan or programme implementation and the effect. Where it is difficult to establish these links it might be necessary to collect further information on plan or programme output indicators (e.g. emissions).

It might also be appropriate to undertake more contextual monitoring of environmental change. This may involve measuring environmental effects or aspects of the environment that were not identified in the environmental assessment, or identifying changes in the broader environmental context. However, this is not required by the Directive.

When selecting indicators to monitor consider how the indicators will be analysed. Emphasis in the monitoring system should be on undertaking proper analysis and interpretation of changes in the indicators, and on identifying the effects of the plan or programme, rather than simply collecting information on large numbers of indicators. Analysis of indictors may include:

- Change in indicators: The effects of plans and programmes can be gauged by examining patterns of change in the indicators and the extent to which related indicators have changed. This can be achieved through analysing groups of indicators together to create a profile of the issue being measured.

- Baselines and predicted effects: Changes and shifts in the direction of indicators should be measured against the baseline position and predicted effects documented in the environmental report.

- Benchmarking: Changes and shifts in the direction of indicators can also be measured against other comparable areas to analyse if similar effects are occurring. Benchmarking may help in the assessment of relative performance by taking into account external forces of change. This is best achieved by establishing a common set of core indicators.

- Use of qualitative and quantitative information: Monitoring of most indicators will be based on the collection of quantitative information. But there may also be a need to incorporate some qualitative information in the analysis to enrich understanding.

- Interpretative commentaries: One task of analysis is providing a considered interpretation of the results. This may be presented via appropriate explanations and commentaries within monitoring reports.

Step 3: What are the existing sources of monitoring information?

Many authorities undertake some form of environmental monitoring. In some cases, the implementation of a plan or programme is monitored against pre-defined objectives, targets and indicators. This type of performance monitoring does not necessarily include environmental effects, unless the Responsible Authority has developed environmental performance indicators or environmental best value indicators. But plan or programme performance monitoring can be helpful when considered together with SEA monitoring. Other existing monitoring is typically focussed on what is required by regulations and legislation (e.g. monitoring required under the Environment Act 1995) but may provide data which is useful either directly or with some degree of analysis or manipulation.

Wherever possible, use existing monitoring arrangements to obtain the required information identified in Step 2. Consider issues such as:

- What are the existing monitoring arrangements for the plan or programme, and does this provide any of the required information?

- What are the existing monitoring arrangements for other plans, programmes or projects within the authority, and is there scope for disaggregating/aggregating data to obtain any of the required information?

- Is any of the required information available from other sources, e.g. higher or lower level authorities or data sources used for establishing the environmental baseline?

- What organisational arrangements are needed to deliver the monitoring?

Step 4: Are there any gaps in the existing information, and how can these be filled?

Additional information collection may be required to monitor those aspects selected in Step 1. Some ways in which the required information can be obtained in a cost-effective and efficient way include:

- Incorporate SEA monitoring into existing performance monitoring for plans and programmes.

- Expand other existing monitoring systems to include additional parameters.

- Where applicable, enter into agreements with other authorities to standardise monitoring methods and share information.

Step 5: What should be done if adverse effects are found?

A Responsible Authority may establish a mechanism or framework to identify if and when remedial action is needed, including:

- Criteria or thresholds for when remedial action is proposed (i.e. what are the conditions that would be regarded environmentally undesirable/unacceptable).

- Potential remedial actions that could be taken if a significant environmental effect was identified (e.g. review aspects of the plan or programme that are causing the effects and make amendments, develop avoidance, mitigation, and enhancement measures).

- Those responsible for taking the remedial action (e.g. another authority or agency may be responsible for taking the remedial action and may need to be consulted).

Step 6: Who is responsible for the various monitoring activities, when should these be carried out, and what is the appropriate format for presenting the monitoring results?

When documenting the monitoring strategy consider:

- the time, frequency and geographical extent of monitoring (e.g link to timeframes for targets; and monitoring whether the effect is predicted to be short, medium or long-term).

- who is responsible for the different monitoring tasks, including the collection, processing and evaluation of environmental information.

- how to present the monitoring information with regard to its purpose and the expertise of those who will have to act upon the information (e.g. information may have to be presented in a form accessible to non-environmental specialists).

Figure 23 suggests a format for documenting out how the monitoring process should be managed.

Figure 23: **Managing the monitoring process**				
Monitoring activity to be undertaken	Who is responsible for undertaking the monitoring?	When should it be carried out (dates and frequency)?	How should the results be presented / appropriate format?	Status / problems encountered

Quality Assurance Checklist

The quality of the SEA process should be assured through the choice of a good SEA team, the collection of appropriate information, the use of effective prediction techniques, consultation, and integration of the SEA findings into the plan or programme. This section suggests a quality assurance checklist based on the guidance in this publication. It is intended to help test whether the requirements of the SEA Directive are met, identify any problems in the Environmental Report, and show how effectively the SEA has integrated environmental considerations into the plan-making process.

The checklist is designed to be used by anyone involved in an SEA in any capacity: Responsible Authorities which carry out SEAs, the organisations which they consult, inspectors, auditors, independent experts, and members of the public. It covers both the technical elements of the SEA and the procedural steps of the SEA process under the Directive. It can be applied at any stage of the SEA to check the quality of work carried out up to that point.

Quality assurance checklist

Objectives and context
- The plan's or programme's purpose and objectives are made clear.
- Environmental issues and constraints, including international and EC environmental protection objectives, are considered in developing objectives and targets.
- SEA objectives, where used, are clearly set out and linked to indicators and targets where appropriate.
- Links with other related plans, programmes and policies are identified and explained.

Scoping
- Consultation Bodies are consulted in appropriate ways and at appropriate times on the content and scope of the Environmental Report.
- The assessment focuses on significant issues.
- Technical, procedural and other difficulties encountered are discussed; assumptions and uncertainties are made explicit.
- Reasons are given for eliminating issues from further consideration.

Alternatives
- Realistic alternatives are considered for key issues, and the reasons for choosing them are documented.
- Alternatives include 'do minimum' and/or 'business as usual' scenarios wherever relevant.
- The environmental effects (both adverse and beneficial) of each alternative are identified and compared.
- Inconsistencies between the alternatives and other relevant plans, programmes or policies are identified and explained.
- Reasons are given for selection or elimination of alternatives.

Baseline information
- Relevant aspects of the current state of the environment and their likely evolution without the plan or programme are described.
- Environmental characteristics of areas likely to be significantly affected are described.
- Difficulties such as deficiencies in information or methods are explained.

Prediction and evaluation of likely significant effects
- Effects identified include the types listed in the Directive (biodiversity, population, human health, fauna, flora, soil, water, air, climate factors, material assets, cultural heritage and landscape), as relevant; other likely effects are also covered.
- Both positive and negative effects are considered, and the duration of effects (short, medium or long-term) is addressed.
- Likely secondary, cumulative and synergistic effects are identified where practicable.
- Inter-relationships between effects are considered where practicable.
- Where relevant, the prediction and evaluation of effects makes use of accepted standards, regulations, and thresholds.
- Methods used to evaluate the effects are described.

Mitigation measures
- Measures envisaged to prevent, reduce and offset any significant adverse effects of implementing the plan or programme are indicated.
- Issues to be taken into account in project consents are identified.

The environmental report
- Is clear and concise in its layout and presentation.
- Uses simple, clear language and avoids or explains technical terms.
- Uses maps and other illustrations where appropriate.
- Explains the methodology used.
- Explains who was consulted and what methods of consultation were used.
- Identifies sources of information, including expert judgement and matters of opinion.
- Contains a non-technical summary covering the overall approach to the SEA, the objectives of the plan, the main options considered, and any changes to the plan resulting from the SEA.

Consultation
- The SEA is consulted on as an integral part of the plan-making process.
- Consultation Bodies and the public likely to be affected by, or having an interest in, the plan or programme are consulted in ways and at times which give them an early and effective opportunity within appropriate time frames to express their opinions on the draft plan and Environmental Report.

Decision-making and information on the decision
- The environmental report and the opinions of those consulted are taken into account in finalising and adopting the plan or programme.
- An explanation is given of how they have been taken into account.
- Reasons are given for choosing the plan or programme as adopted, in the light of other reasonable alternatives considered.

Monitoring measures
- Measures proposed for monitoring are clear, practicable and linked to the indicators and objectives used in the SEA.
- During implementation of the plan or programme, monitoring is used where appropriate to make good deficiencies in baseline information in the SEA.
- Monitoring enables unforeseen adverse effects to be identified at an early stage. (These effects should include predictions which prove to be incorrect.)
- Proposals are made for action in response to significant adverse effects.

References and Further Information

Audit Commission (2000). **Listen up! Effective Community Consultation**.
Audit Commission, London
http://ww2.audit-commission.gov.uk/publications/pdf/mpeffect.pdf

Canadian Environmental Assessment Agency (1999). **Addressing Cumulative
Environmental Effects**. CEAA, Gatineau, Quebec
http://www.ceaa-acee.gc.ca/0011/0001/0008/guide1_e.htm.

Chambers, N., Simmons, C. and Wackernagel, M. (2000). **Sharing Nature's
Interest**. Earthscan, London.

Countryside Agency et al (2001). **Quality of Life Capital: overview report**.
Countryside Agency, Cheltenham
http://www.qualityoflifecapital.org.uk

David Tyldesley and Associates (August 2003). **Environmental Assessment of
Development Plans: Interim Planning Advice**. Scottish Executive Social Research

Department of the Environment, Transport and the Regions (1999). **A Better Quality
of Life: A strategy for sustainable development for the UK**. TSO, London
http://www.sustainable-development.gov.uk/uk_strategy/content.htm

Department of the Environment, Transport and the Regions (1999). **Quality of Life
Counts: Indicators for a strategy for sustainable development for the UK –
a baseline assessment**. DETR, London
http://www.sustainable-development.gov.uk/sustainable/quality99/

Department of the Environment, Transport and the Regions (2000). **Local Quality
of Life Counts: a handbook for a menu of local indicators of sustainable
development**. DETR, London
http://www.sustainable-development.gov.uk/indicators/local/localind/index.htm

Department of the Environment, Transport and the Regions (2000). **Multi Criteria
Analysis: A Manual**. DETR, London
http://www.odpm.gov.uk/stellent/groups/odpm_about/documents/page/odpm_
about_608524.

Department of the Environment, Food and Rural Affairs (Sustainable Development
Unit) (2002). **Regional Quality of Life Counts**.
http://www.sustainable-development.gov.uk/indicators/regional/2002/

European Commission (2003). **Implementation of Directive 2001/42 on the
assessment of the effects of certain plans and programmes on the
environment**. Commission of the European Communities, Brussels
http://europa.eu.int/comm/environment/eia/030923_sea_guidance.pdf

European Commission, (2001). **SEA and Integration of the Environment into Strategic Decision-Making**. ICON, London
http://europa.eu.int/comm/environment/eia/sea-support.htm

European Commission (1999). **Guidelines for the Assessment of Indirect and Cumulative Impacts as well as Impact Interactions**. Commission of the European Communities, Brussels
http://europa.eu.int/comm/environment/eia/eia-studies-and-reports/guidel.htm

European Environment Agency (1998). **Spatial and Ecological Assessment of the TEN: Demonstration of Indicators and GIS Methods**. Environmental Issues Series No. 11 EAA, Copenhagen
http://reports.eea.eu.int/GH-15-98-318-EN-C/en

European Parliament and Council of the European Union (2001). **Directive 2001/42/EC on the assessment of the effects of certain plans and programmes on the environment**. Commission of the European Communities, Brussels
http://europa.eu.int/eur-lex/pri/en/oj/dat/2001/l_197/l_19720010721en00300037.pdf

Institute of Environmental Management and Assessment (IEMA) (2002). **Perspectives: Guidelines on participation in environmental decision-making**. IEMA, Lincoln.

Levett-Therivel (2002). **Implementing the SEA Directive: Analysis of Existing Practice**. Report to the South-West Regional Assembly.
http://www.southwest-ra.gov.uk/swra/ourwork/environment/sea.shtml

Levett-Therivel (2003). **Implementing the SEA Directive: Five Pilot Studies**. Report to the South-West Regional Assembly.
http://www.southwest-ra.gov.uk/swra/ourwork/environment/sea.shtml

Smith, S.P. and W.R. Sheate (2001a). **Sustainability appraisal of English regional plans: incorporating the requirements of the EU Strategic Environmental Assessment Directive**. Impact Assessment and Project Appraisal, 19(4), December 2001, pp. 263-276.

Smith, S.P. and W.R. Sheate (2001b). **Sustainability appraisal of Regional Planning Guidance and Regional Economic Strategies in England: An Assessment**. Journal of Environmental Planning and Management 44(5), September 2001, pp. 735-755.

TRL Ltd and Collingwood Environmental Planning (2002). **Analysis of Baseline Data Requirements for the SEA Directive – Final Report**.
http://www.trl.co.uk/static/environment/SWRA%20SEA%20Report%2011.pdf

Wates, Nick (Ed.) (2000). **The Community Planning Handbook**, Earthscan Publications Ltd, London.

The SEA Directive

L 197/30 | EN | Official Journal of the European Communities | 21.7.2001

DIRECTIVE 2001/42/EC OF THE EUROPEAN PARLIAMENT AND OF THE COUNCIL
of 27 June 2001
on the assessment of the effects of certain plans and programmes on the environment

THE EUROPEAN PARLIAMENT AND THE COUNCIL OF THE EUROPEAN UNION,

Having regard to the Treaty establishing the European Community, and in particular Article 175(1) thereof,

Having regard to the proposal from the Commission (¹),

Having regard to the opinion of the Economic and Social Committee (²),

Having regard to the opinion of the Committee of the Regions (³),

Acting in accordance with the procedure laid down in Article 251 of the Treaty (⁴), in the light of the joint text approved by the Conciliation Committee on 21 March 2001,

Whereas:

(1) Article 174 of the Treaty provides that Community policy on the environment is to contribute to, *inter alia*, the preservation, protection and improvement of the quality of the environment, the protection of human health and the prudent and rational utilisation of natural resources and that it is to be based on the precautionary principle. Article 6 of the Treaty provides that environmental protection requirements are to be integrated into the definition of Community policies and activities, in particular with a view to promoting sustainable development.

(2) The Fifth Environment Action Programme: Towards sustainability — A European Community programme of policy and action in relation to the environment and sustainable development (⁵), supplemented by Council Decision No 2179/98/EC (⁶) on its review, affirms the importance of assessing the likely environmental effects of plans and programmes.

(3) The Convention on Biological Diversity requires Parties to integrate as far as possible and as appropriate the conservation and sustainable use of biological diversity into relevant sectoral or cross-sectoral plans and programmes.

(4) Environmental assessment is an important tool for integrating environmental considerations into the preparation and adoption of certain plans and programmes which are likely to have significant effects on the environment in the Member States, because it ensures that such effects of implementing plans and programmes are taken into account during their preparation and before their adoption.

(5) The adoption of environmental assessment procedures at the planning and programming level should benefit undertakings by providing a more consistent framework in which to operate by the inclusion of the relevant environmental information into decision making. The inclusion of a wider set of factors in decision making should contribute to more sustainable and effective solutions.

(6) The different environmental assessment systems operating within Member States should contain a set of common procedural requirements necessary to contribute to a high level of protection of the environment.

(7) The United Nations/Economic Commission for Europe Convention on Environmental Impact Assessment in a Transboundary Context of 25 February 1991, which applies to both Member States and other States, encourages the parties to the Convention to apply its principles to plans and programmes as well; at the second meeting of the Parties to the Convention in Sofia on 26 and 27 February 2001, it was decided to prepare a legally binding protocol on strategic environmental assessment which would supplement the existing provisions on environmental impact assessment in a transboundary context, with a view to its possible adoption on the occasion of the 5th Ministerial Conference 'Environment for Europe' at an extraordinary meeting of the Parties to the Convention, scheduled for May 2003 in Kiev, Ukraine. The systems operating within the Community for environmental assessment of plans and programmes should ensure that there are adequate transboundary consultations where the implementation of a plan or programme being prepared in one Member State is likely to have significant effects on the environment of another Member State. The information on plans and programmes having significant effects on the environment of other States should be forwarded on a reciprocal and equivalent basis within an appropriate legal framework between Member States and these other States.

(¹) OJ C 129, 25.4.1997, p. 14 and
    OJ C 83, 25.3.1999, p. 13.
(²) OJ C 287, 22.9.1997, p. 101.
(³) OJ C 64, 27.2.1998, p. 63 and
    OJ C 374, 23.12.1999, p. 9.
(⁴) Opinion of the European Parliament of 20 October 1998 (OJ C 341, 9.11.1998, p. 18), confirmed on 16 September 1999 (OJ C 54, 25.2.2000, p. 76), Council Common Position of 30 March 2000 (OJ C 137, 16.5.2000, p. 11) and Decision of the European Parliament of 6 September 2000 (OJ C 135, 7.5.2001, p. 155). Decision of the European Parliament of 31 May 2001 and Decision of the Council of 5 June 2001.
(⁵) OJ C 138, 17.5.1993, p. 5.
(⁶) OJ L 275, 10.10.1998, p. 1.

21.7.2001   EN   Official Journal of the European Communities   L 197/31

(8) Action is therefore required at Community level to lay down a minimum environmental assessment framework, which would set out the broad principles of the environmental assessment system and leave the details to the Member States, having regard to the principle of subsidiarity. Action by the Community should not go beyond what is necessary to achieve the objectives set out in the Treaty.

(9) This Directive is of a procedural nature, and its requirements should either be integrated into existing procedures in Member States or incorporated in specifically established procedures. With a view to avoiding duplication of the assessment, Member States should take account, where appropriate, of the fact that assessments will be carried out at different levels of a hierarchy of plans and programmes.

(10) All plans and programmes which are prepared for a number of sectors and which set a framework for future development consent of projects listed in Annexes I and II to Council Directive 85/337/EEC of 27 June 1985 on the assessment of the effects of certain public and private projects on the environment (¹), and all plans and programmes which have been determined to require assessment pursuant to Council Directive 92/43/EEC of 21 May 1992 on the conservation of natural habitats and of wild flora and fauna (²), are likely to have significant effects on the environment, and should as a rule be made subject to systematic environmental assessment. When they determine the use of small areas at local level or are minor modifications to the above plans or programmes, they should be assessed only where Member States determine that they are likely to have significant effects on the environment.

(11) Other plans and programmes which set the framework for future development consent of projects may not have significant effects on the environment in all cases and should be assessed only where Member States determine that they are likely to have such effects.

(12) When Member States make such determinations, they should take into account the relevant criteria set out in this Directive.

(13) Some plans or programmes are not subject to this Directive because of their particular characteristics.

(14) Where an assessment is required by this Directive, an environmental report should be prepared containing relevant information as set out in this Directive, identifying, describing and evaluating the likely significant environmental effects of implementing the plan or programme, and reasonable alternatives taking into account the objectives and the geographical scope of the plan or programme; Member States should communi-

cate to the Commission any measures they take concerning the quality of environmental reports.

(15) In order to contribute to more transparent decision making and with the aim of ensuring that the information supplied for the assessment is comprehensive and reliable, it is necessary to provide that authorities with relevant environmental responsibilities and the public are to be consulted during the assessment of plans and programmes, and that appropriate time frames are set, allowing sufficient time for consultations, including the expression of opinion.

(16) Where the implementation of a plan or programme prepared in one Member State is likely to have a significant effect on the environment of other Member States, provision should be made for the Member States concerned to enter into consultations and for the relevant authorities and the public to be informed and enabled to express their opinion.

(17) The environmental report and the opinions expressed by the relevant authorities and the public, as well as the results of any transboundary consultation, should be taken into account during the preparation of the plan or programme and before its adoption or submission to the legislative procedure.

(18) Member States should ensure that, when a plan or programme is adopted, the relevant authorities and the public are informed and relevant information is made available to them.

(19) Where the obligation to carry out assessments of the effects on the environment arises simultaneously from this Directive and other Community legislation, such as Council Directive 79/409/EEC of 2 April 1979 on the conservation of wild birds (³), Directive 92/43/EEC, or Directive 2000/60/EC of the European Parliament and the Council of 23 October 2000 establishing a framework for Community action in the field of water policy (⁴), in order to avoid duplication of the assessment, Member States may provide for coordinated or joint procedures fulfilling the requirements of the relevant Community legislation.

(20) A first report on the application and effectiveness of this Directive should be carried out by the Commission five years after its entry into force, and at seven-year intervals thereafter. With a view to further integrating environmental protection requirements, and taking into account the experience acquired, the first report should, if appropriate, be accompanied by proposals for amendment of this Directive, in particular as regards the possibility of extending its scope to other areas/sectors and other types of plans and programmes,

(¹) OJ L 175, 5.7.1985, p. 40. Directive as amended by Directive 97/11/EC (OJ L 73, 14.3.1997, p. 5).
(²) OJ L 206, 22.7.1992, p. 7. Directive as last amended by Directive 97/62/EC (OJ L 305, 8.11.1997, p. 42).

(³) OJ L 103, 25.4.1979, p. 1. Directive as last amended by Directive 97/49/EC (OJ L 223, 13.8.1997, p. 9).
(⁴) OJ L 327, 22.12.2000, p. 1.

HAVE ADOPTED THIS DIRECTIVE:

Article 1

Objectives

The objective of this Directive is to provide for a high level of protection of the environment and to contribute to the integration of environmental considerations into the preparation and adoption of plans and programmes with a view to promoting sustainable development, by ensuring that, in accordance with this Directive, an environmental assessment is carried out of certain plans and programmes which are likely to have significant effects on the environment.

Article 2

Definitions

For the purposes of this Directive:

(a) 'plans and programmes' shall mean plans and programmes, including those co-financed by the European Community, as well as any modifications to them:

— which are subject to preparation and/or adoption by an authority at national, regional or local level or which are prepared by an authority for adoption, through a legislative procedure by Parliament or Government, and

— which are required by legislative, regulatory or administrative provisions;

(b) 'environmental assessment' shall mean the preparation of an environmental report, the carrying out of consultations, the taking into account of the environmental report and the results of the consultations in decision-making and the provision of information on the decision in accordance with Articles 4 to 9;

(c) 'environmental report' shall mean the part of the plan or programme documentation containing the information required in Article 5 and Annex I;

(d) 'The public' shall mean one or more natural or legal persons and, in accordance with national legislation or practice, their associations, organisations or groups.

Article 3

Scope

1. An environmental assessment, in accordance with Articles 4 to 9, shall be carried out for plans and programmes referred to in paragraphs 2 to 4 which are likely to have significant environmental effects.

2. Subject to paragraph 3, an environmental assessment shall be carried out for all plans and programmes,

(a) which are prepared for agriculture, forestry, fisheries, energy, industry, transport, waste management, water management, telecommunications, tourism, town and country planning or land use and which set the framework for future development consent of projects listed in Annexes I and II to Directive 85/337/EEC, or

(b) which, in view of the likely effect on sites, have been determined to require an assessment pursuant to Article 6 or 7 of Directive 92/43/EEC.

3. Plans and programmes referred to in paragraph 2 which determine the use of small areas at local level and minor modifications to plans and programmes referred to in paragraph 2 shall require an environmental assessment only where the Member States determine that they are likely to have significant environmental effects.

4. Member States shall determine whether plans and programmes, other than those referred to in paragraph 2, which set the framework for future development consent of projects, are likely to have significant environmental effects.

5. Member States shall determine whether plans or programmes referred to in paragraphs 3 and 4 are likely to have significant environmental effects either through case-by-case examination or by specifying types of plans and programmes or by combining both approaches. For this purpose Member States shall in all cases take into account relevant criteria set out in Annex II, in order to ensure that plans and programmes with likely significant effects on the environment are covered by this Directive.

6. In the case-by-case examination and in specifying types of plans and programmes in accordance with paragraph 5, the authorities referred to in Article 6(3) shall be consulted.

7. Member States shall ensure that their conclusions pursuant to paragraph 5, including the reasons for not requiring an environmental assessment pursuant to Articles 4 to 9, are made available to the public.

8. The following plans and programmes are not subject to this Directive:

— plans and programmes the sole purpose of which is to serve national defence or civil emergency,

— financial or budget plans and programmes.

9. This Directive does not apply to plans and programmes co-financed under the current respective programming periods (¹) for Council Regulations (EC) No 1260/1999 (²) and (EC) No 1257/1999 (³).

(¹) The 2000-2006 programming period for Council Regulation (EC) No 1260/1999 and the 2000-2006 and 2000-2007 programming periods for Council Regulation (EC) No 1257/1999.
(²) Council Regulation (EC) No 1260/1999 of 21 June 1999 laying down general provisions on the Structural Funds (OJ L 161, 26.6.1999, p. 1).
(³) Council Regulation (EC) No 1257/1999 of 17 May 1999 on support for rural development from the European Agricultural Guidance and Guarantee Fund (EAGGF) and amending and repealing certain regulations (OJ L 160, 26.6.1999, p. 80).

21.7.2001 · EN · Official Journal of the European Communities · L 197/33

Article 4

General obligations

1. The environmental assessment referred to in Article 3 shall be carried out during the preparation of a plan or programme and before its adoption or submission to the legislative procedure.

2. The requirements of this Directive shall either be integrated into existing procedures in Member States for the adoption of plans and programmes or incorporated in procedures established to comply with this Directive.

3. Where plans and programmes form part of a hierarchy, Member States shall, with a view to avoiding duplication of the assessment, take into account the fact that the assessment will be carried out, in accordance with this Directive, at different levels of the hierarchy. For the purpose of, *inter alia*, avoiding duplication of assessment, Member States shall apply Article 5(2) and (3).

Article 5

Environmental report

1. Where an environmental assessment is required under Article 3(1), an environmental report shall be prepared in which the likely significant effects on the environment of implementing the plan or programme, and reasonable alternatives taking into account the objectives and the geographical scope of the plan or programme, are identified, described and evaluated. The information to be given for this purpose is referred to in Annex I.

2. The environmental report prepared pursuant to paragraph 1 shall include the information that may reasonably be required taking into account current knowledge and methods of assessment, the contents and level of detail in the plan or programme, its stage in the decision-making process and the extent to which certain matters are more appropriately assessed at different levels in that process in order to avoid duplication of the assessment.

3. Relevant information available on environmental effects of the plans and programmes and obtained at other levels of decision-making or through other Community legislation may be used for providing the information referred to in Annex I.

4. The authorities referred to in Article 6(3) shall be consulted when deciding on the scope and level of detail of the information which must be included in the environmental report.

Article 6

Consultations

1. The draft plan or programme and the environmental report prepared in accordance with Article 5 shall be made available to the authorities referred to in paragraph 3 of this Article and the public.

2. The authorities referred to in paragraph 3 and the public referred to in paragraph 4 shall be given an early and effective opportunity within appropriate time frames to express their opinion on the draft plan or programme and the accompanying environmental report before the adoption of the plan or programme or its submission to the legislative procedure.

3. Member States shall designate the authorities to be consulted which, by reason of their specific environmental responsibilities, are likely to be concerned by the environmental effects of implementing plans and programmes.

4. Member States shall identify the public for the purposes of paragraph 2, including the public affected or likely to be affected by, or having an interest in, the decision-making subject to this Directive, including relevant non-governmental organisations, such as those promoting environmental protection and other organisations concerned.

5. The detailed arrangements for the information and consultation of the authorities and the public shall be determined by the Member States.

Article 7

Transboundary consultations

1. Where a Member State considers that the implementation of a plan or programme being prepared in relation to its territory is likely to have significant effects on the environment in another Member State, or where a Member State likely to be significantly affected so requests, the Member State in whose territory the plan or programme is being prepared shall, before its adoption or submission to the legislative procedure, forward a copy of the draft plan or programme and the relevant environmental report to the other Member State.

2. Where a Member State is sent a copy of a draft plan or programme and an environmental report under paragraph 1, it shall indicate to the other Member State whether it wishes to enter into consultations before the adoption of the plan or programme or its submission to the legislative procedure and, if it so indicates, the Member States concerned shall enter into consultations concerning the likely transboundary environmental effects of implementing the plan or programme and the measures envisaged to reduce or eliminate such effects.

Where such consultations take place, the Member States concerned shall agree on detailed arrangements to ensure that the authorities referred to in Article 6(3) and the public referred to in Article 6(4) in the Member State likely to be significantly affected are informed and given an opportunity to forward their opinion within a reasonable time-frame.

3. Where Member States are required under this Article to enter into consultations, they shall agree, at the beginning of such consultations, on a reasonable timeframe for the duration of the consultations.

Article 8

Decision making

The environmental report prepared pursuant to Article 5, the opinions expressed pursuant to Article 6 and the results of any transboundary consultations entered into pursuant to Article 7 shall be taken into account during the preparation of the plan or programme and before its adoption or submission to the legislative procedure.

Article 9

Information on the decision

1. Member States shall ensure that, when a plan or programme is adopted, the authorities referred to in Article 6(3), the public and any Member State consulted under Article 7 are informed and the following items are made available to those so informed:

(a) the plan or programme as adopted;

(b) a statement summarising how environmental considerations have been integrated into the plan or programme and how the environmental report prepared pursuant to Article 5, the opinions expressed pursuant to Article 6 and the results of consultations entered into pursuant to Article 7 have been taken into account in accordance with Article 8 and the reasons for choosing the plan or programme as adopted, in the light of the other reasonable alternatives dealt with, and

(c) the measures decided concerning monitoring in accordance with Article 10.

2. The detailed arrangements concerning the information referred to in paragraph 1 shall be determined by the Member States.

Article 10

Monitoring

1. Member States shall monitor the significant environmental effects of the implementation of plans and programmes in order, inter alia, to identify at an early stage unforeseen adverse effects, and to be able to undertake appropriate remedial action.

2. In order to comply with paragraph 1, existing monitoring arrangements may be used if appropriate, with a view to avoiding duplication of monitoring.

Article 11

Relationship with other Community legislation

1. An environmental assessment carried out under this Directive shall be without prejudice to any requirements under Directive 85/337/EEC and to any other Community law requirements.

2. For plans and programmes for which the obligation to carry out assessments of the effects on the environment arises simultaneously from this Directive and other Community legislation, Member States may provide for coordinated or joint procedures fulfilling the requirements of the relevant Community legislation in order, inter alia, to avoid duplication of assessment.

3. For plans and programmes co-financed by the European Community, the environmental assessment in accordance with this Directive shall be carried out in conformity with the specific provisions in relevant Community legislation.

Article 12

Information, reporting and review

1. Member States and the Commission shall exchange information on the experience gained in applying this Directive.

2. Member States shall ensure that environmental reports are of a sufficient quality to meet the requirements of this Directive and shall communicate to the Commission any measures they take concerning the quality of these reports.

3. Before 21 July 2006 the Commission shall send a first report on the application and effectiveness of this Directive to the European Parliament and to the Council.

With a view further to integrating environmental protection requirements, in accordance with Article 6 of the Treaty, and taking into account the experience acquired in the application of this Directive in the Member States, such a report will be accompanied by proposals for amendment of this Directive, if appropriate. In particular, the Commission will consider the possibility of extending the scope of this Directive to other areas/sectors and other types of plans and programmes.

A new evaluation report shall follow at seven-year intervals.

4. The Commission shall report on the relationship between this Directive and Regulations (EC) No 1260/1999 and (EC) No 1257/1999 well ahead of the expiry of the programming periods provided for in those Regulations, with a view to ensuring a coherent approach with regard to this Directive and subsequent Community Regulations.

Article 13

Implementation of the Directive

1. Member States shall bring into force the laws, regulations and administrative provisions necessary to comply with this Directive before 21 July 2004. They shall forthwith inform the Commission thereof.

2. When Member States adopt the measures, they shall contain a reference to this Directive or shall be accompanied by such reference on the occasion of their official publication. The methods of making such reference shall be laid down by Member States.

3. The obligation referred to in Article 4(1) shall apply to the plans and programmes of which the first formal preparatory act is subsequent to the date referred to in paragraph 1. Plans and programmes of which the first formal preparatory act is before that date and which are adopted or submitted to the legislative procedure more than 24 months thereafter, shall be made subject to the obligation referred to in Article 4(1) unless Member States decide on a case by case basis that this is not feasible and inform the public of their decision.

4. Before 21 July 2004, Member States shall communicate to the Commission, in addition to the measures referred to in paragraph 1, separate information on the types of plans and programmes which, in accordance with Article 3, would be subject to an environmental assessment pursuant to this Directive. The Commission shall make this information available to the Member States. The information will be updated on a regular basis.

Article 14

Entry into force

This Directive shall enter into force on the day of its publication in the *Official Journal of the European Communities*.

Article 15

Addressees

This Directive is addressed to the Member States.

Done at Luxembourg, 27 June 2001.

For the European Parliament	*For the Council*
The President	*The President*
N. FONTAINE	B. ROSENGREN

ANNEX I

Information referred to in Article 5(1)

The information to be provided under Article 5(1), subject to Article 5(2) and (3), is the following:

(a) an outline of the contents, main objectives of the plan or programme and relationship with other relevant plans and programmes;

(b) the relevant aspects of the current state of the environment and the likely evolution thereof without implementation of the plan or programme;

(c) the environmental characteristics of areas likely to be significantly affected;

(d) any existing environmental problems which are relevant to the plan or programme including, in particular, those relating to any areas of a particular environmental importance, such as areas designated pursuant to Directives 79/409/EEC and 92/43/EEC;

(e) the environmental protection objectives, established at international, Community or Member State level, which are relevant to the plan or programme and the way those objectives and any environmental considerations have been taken into account during its preparation;

(f) the likely significant effects ([1]) on the environment, including on issues such as biodiversity, population, human health, fauna, flora, soil, water, air, climatic factors, material assets, cultural heritage including architectural and archaeological heritage, landscape and the interrelationship between the above factors;

(g) the measures envisaged to prevent, reduce and as fully as possible offset any significant adverse effects on the environment of implementing the plan or programme;

(h) an outline of the reasons for selecting the alternatives dealt with, and a description of how the assessment was undertaken including any difficulties (such as technical deficiencies or lack of know-how) encountered in compiling the required information;

(i) a description of the measures envisaged concerning monitoring in accordance with Article 10;

(j) a non-technical summary of the information provided under the above headings.

————

([1]) These effects should include secondary, cumulative, synergistic, short, medium and long-term permanent and temporary, positive and negative effects.

21.7.2001   EN   Official Journal of the European Communities   L 197/37

ANNEX II

Criteria for determining the likely significance of effects referred to in Article 3(5)

1. The characteristics of plans and programmes, having regard, in particular, to
   - the degree to which the plan or programme sets a framework for projects and other activities, either with regard to the location, nature, size and operating conditions or by allocating resources,
   - the degree to which the plan or programme influences other plans and programmes including those in a hierarchy,
   - the relevance of the plan or programme for the integration of environmental considerations in particular with a view to promoting sustainable development,
   - environmental problems relevant to the plan or programme,
   - the relevance of the plan or programme for the implementation of Community legislation on the environment (e.g. plans and programmes linked to waste-management or water protection).

2. Characteristics of the effects and of the area likely to be affected, having regard, in particular, to
   - the probability, duration, frequency and reversibility of the effects,
   - the cumulative nature of the effects,
   - the transboundary nature of the effects,
   - the risks to human health or the environment (e.g. due to accidents),
   - the magnitude and spatial extent of the effects (geographical area and size of the population likely to be affected),
   - the value and vulnerability of the area likely to be affected due to:
     - special natural characteristics or cultural heritage,
     - exceeded environmental quality standards or limit values,
     - intensive land-use,
   - the effects on areas or landscapes which have a recognised national, Community or international protection status.